KATE BUSH

KATE BUSH

The Whole Story

Kerry Juby
with Karen Sullivan

SIDGWICK & JACKSON
LONDON

First published in October 1988 by
Sidgwick & Jackson Limited
1 Tavistock Chambers, Bloomsbury Way
London WC1A 2SG

First Reprint December 1988
Second Reprint February 1989

ISBN 0-283-99721-4

Typeset by Hewer Text Composition Services, Edinburgh
Printed in Great Britain by Butler & Tanner Limited
Frome, Somerset
for Sidgwick & Jackson Limited
1 Tavistock Chambers,
Bloomsbury Way
London WC1A 2SG

*To Margaret and Roo
and to Poppy for
patience*

CONTENTS

ACKNOWLEDGEMENTS

Many thanks to everyone who has been so helpful and so utterly patient. The book could not have happened without them. For remembering all the little details, thanks to: Kate Bush, Max Middleton, Alan Murphy, Simon Drake, Andrew Powell, Stuart Elliot, Steve Harley, Richard Aimes, Hilary Walker, Frances Byrne, Martin Montgomery, Sarah Craddy, Tony Myatt, Eddie Puma, Lindsay Kemp, Antony van Laast, and Jon Kelly. For coming up with facts where there just didn't seem to be any: Chris Kelly, Kevin Cann, Mary Finnigan, Peter Sternburg, Linda Griffiths, *Melody Maker*, The Kate Bush Club, Homeground, EMI, *NME* and *The Record Collector*. Thanks also to *The Times*, the *Evening Standard*, *Daily Mirror*, *Daily Express* and *Company*.

And to the people who made all the words come together: Karen Hurrell, Paul Iddiols, Anne Cohen and very special thanks to Juliet Van Oss.

PROLOGUE

Any attempt to discover the secret life of Kate Bush would be nonsensical, for no such life exists. Certainly the most difficult facet of any Kate Bush analysis is the secrecy that surrounds her personal life: however, it is a healthy secrecy, and one that normal people adhere to religiously. Kate Bush is, in fact, one of the most normal, the most cordial and the most genuine musicians on the rock scene today. She is consistently ranked with the very best of the music world; her public expect to discover the same sort of hedonism and heresy that personifies many of the legendary artists, but they draw a blank. There is no such side to Kate Bush. Friends, family and colleagues are protective and almost maternal about her, but there is no doubt that the concensus remains entirely conclusive: Kate Bush is a nice and incredibly down-to-earth person.

Kate fills a gap in many lives with her music and with the poetics and theatrics that accompany it. She is truly well loved. Gregarious, helpful and very sane, facts of her nature that none dares nor has any wish to contradict, Kate has charmed a nation, and through that, the world. She is the nice girl of pop, the girl you could take home to Mum, with talents that are undoubtedly multifarious.

This book originally intended to discover the true Kate Bush, the one who has hidden herself so well from the public eye in the shadow of her music and, paradoxically, her stage presence. Happily, no such self exists. Kate Bush remains today the very same girl who astounded the music world in her teens. Kate Bush's life *is* her music, and her focus is the people that surround it and her. To delve into her personal life, something that she feels most strongly should be kept separate from the business, would be a travesty, an insult to Kate Bush and her music. As it happens there just isn't anything there to discover. Kate Bush writes music. Then she records it and promotes it as a product, enlivening it with the sense of drama and dance that is so very characteristic of her personality. She lives a normal, balanced life with her boyfriend and her family. There is absolutely no façade. The Kate Bush portrayed to the public through the channels of EMI or through Kate herself is no different from the Kate Bush that exists at home.

This is the story of Kate Bush, from her beginnings to the present day. It is a celebration of her music, and of the person behind the music as she appears to her friends and the people she works with. The undisputed concensus is that to know Kate is to love her.

1

IN THE WINGS

Warm and soothing
That's how I remember home
Walking into arms through the back door
Hearing voices I know well and long for
                    'Warm and Soothing'
                        Kate Bush, 1980

Tucked away from the cement suburbia that flanks the main London to Dover motorway lies the small but lively town of Welling in Kent. Rolling hills and early Victorian architecture contrast sharply with the more modern developments that have sprouted up over the past few decades, but the community has retained a great deal of its rural charm. It was here that Kate Bush grew up – in a 350-year-old farmhouse nestling in the hills that overlook the Woolwich cemetery. The farmhouse itself is hidden from the road and from the crop of small businesses and flats that has developed in the surrounding streets. Nine-foot walls encompass the grounds while wild and unkempt greenery winds and curls over the grey and weatherbeaten brick façade of ancient East Wickham Farm. A fish-pond and an old Tudor barn complete the idyllic scenery of the old-fashioned haven.

Robert Bush, Kate's father, was an exceptionally bright student who was studying for a degree in mathematics when the Second World War changed his thinking: 'It did seem somewhat aimless . . . and medicine has always been my passion.' He proceeded to win a scholarship to Grays Grammar School, where he excelled in his exams for medical school. After graduating in 1943 he married Kate's mother, Hannah Daly, who was a senior staff nurse at Long Grove Hospital in Epsom. Three years older than him, Hannah was the daughter of an Irish Catholic farmer. Shortly after their marriage Dr Bush joined the army and was shipped to India. When the war ended, the Bushes took up residence in Welling, where Dr Bush worked until recently with a practice of over seven thousand patients in a thriving partnership with three other GPs.

Born Catherine Bush on 30th July 1958 at Bexleyheath Maternity Hospital, Kate's childhood was a normal one. She was the youngest of the three Bush children and was nicknamed 'Cathy' by her parents and two older brothers, Paddy and John. East Wickham Farm was a natural playground for the three children and Kate spent countless hours there with school friends and her brothers. Frances Byrne, a school friend, recalls: 'Most of our time was spent at her parents' house. The house itself is a farmhouse type of building and I remember it being very, very big. It must have been eight bedrooms from what I remember although I wasn't, naturally, very impressed at the time. Outside in the grounds there was quite a large barn, a dovecot, and Kate had a playhouse which was a Tudor-style Wendy house made of wood. All the windows were glazed and it had little doors that locked.' Kate adds: 'I joined in all my brothers' games when I was younger and they'd always end up tying me to a tree or something!' Kate also amused herself in her spare hours by adorning herself in a variety of jumble sale costumes to playact, pose for pictures and dance for her parents.

Early pictures of Kate show her as a cheerful if somewhat intense child – tiny elfin features topped with the same mop of tangled auburn hair that characterizes her today. The family was and is a very close one, and her childhood was fairly sheltered. Frances Byrne goes on: 'Her father used to drive her everywhere. I wouldn't say that her childhood was cocooned in any way; perhaps well-protected would be a better way of describing it – that is, well-protected with a lot of freedom. I can never remember her saying "I can't do such and such because I am not allowed".' The family unit, even in the early days, was incredibly important to Kate, as it was to all the Bushes. Most of her friends remember thinking it odd that Kate was so entirely comfortable with them that she spent all her spare time in their company. It doesn't seem that her family were in any way restrictive; in fact the amount of freedom that she was given at a very early age was probably one of the factors that allowed her creativity to develop. Another friend remembers, 'One of the things that always struck me about the family was that her mother always seemed to be around but didn't tell Kate what to do. In fact, the whole family seemed very easy-going . . . she was given a great deal of freedom to develop in any direction she felt she wanted to.' Kate is remembered as always having a great deal of pocket money. She never went short of anything she really wanted, which suggests that the young Kate Bush was rather spoilt; but her childhood friends jump quickly to her defence. Frances Byrne comments: 'She wasn't the sort of person to have temper tantrums or to be dreadfully selfish'. It appears that the general characteristics of Kate's personality which make her so popular with her friends today precluded anything but sterling behaviour.

Kate's mother led the family unit with an iron hand, and is remembered as being a stolid, good-natured woman who had faith in the innate common sense of her children and their ability to choose their own paths. Dr Bush was similarly even-tempered and extremely generous, finding plenty of pocket money for his own children, and apparently also for anyone else's who happened to be there at the time. He was less inclined to be the disciplinary force in the family, leaving such measures to his wife, who was capable of a sterner temperament. Kate's friends, however, do not recall ever witnessing a need for discipline – Kate had an extraordinary respect for her brothers and her parents and did not appear to go through the rebellious stage that many children do.

For many of her early years her elder brother by fourteen years, John Carder, (nicknamed Jay) was not present, but Paddy, who was eight years older than her did spend a considerable amount of time around the house and was therefore in a position where he could have been a role model for Kate. Frances describes Paddy as being, 'a vague sort of person. A lot of the time he was in his room and when he was there, writing or composing or playing his instruments, nobody was allowed to disturb him. He also wrote poetry I remember. In fact, at one time he described himself as a poet.' Evidently there were no pressures in the Bush household to conform to a predetermined profession. Dr Bush never expected his sons to become doctors; rather, the natural gifts of each were encouraged

3

and supported no end, no matter how abstract or odd they seemed at the time.

From her twelfth year, Kate attended St Joseph's Convent School at Abbey Wood, not far from her home, and it was here that her gift for poetry was recognized. The school is described as being a very old building with a new, much more clinical addition that had been built on at a much later date. Frances enlarges upon this; 'The old part was a rather dismal building, very Victorian looking, an old red-brick building with trees lined along the front of it, and wooden desks and fitments that tended to go along with those older sorts of schools.' The uniform was a maroon blazer, skirt and tie with regulation brown shoes, strictly adhered to under the auspices of the nuns. Despite its being a Roman Catholic convent, the school had a reputation for being freethinking. Although religious education was part of the curriculum, the students were encouraged to develop their own ideas and concepts. A schoolfriend Sarah Craddy, notes: 'It was difficult to forget religion existed with nuns dotted about everywhere, but I suppose that's why you attend that sort of school. In many ways it can be a very insular form of education. There always used to be some sort of prayer before every lesson, but apart from that, lessons would be fairly free, except religious education that is, when we had to read the bible and explain what it means.'

Kate is remembered as being a shy person, but one who was always surrounded by a small group of friends. Sarah continues: 'She didn't seem to be the sort of person who was totally happy with her own company; she did like to have a little group around her so there was always someone there. In a perverse sort of way, she was insular in that she didn't mix with the whole of the class. She was always a quiet type of girl and seemed to keep in the midstream at school, so I can't remember her being particularly wonderful or, for that matter, awful at anything. During that period she spent a lot of her spare time at home. And her dad would pick her up each evening after school and take her home.' Kate also describes herself as quiet: 'I think I was quite a shy person. It was just a straight school. There wasn't much concern about self-expression in an artistic way. There were music and dancing classes, but there wasn't very much concentration on that – it was much more on maths, biology. I think

I learnt a few things from school which were useful, but generally it wasn't an environment that I felt I could express myself in – because I was shy, I think.'

Aside from her propensity to write reams of poetry and to compose at an early age, Kate had rather different aspirations in her younger years than her memories suggest. She was interested for a long time in becoming a veterinary surgeon, but upon discovering the prerequisite sciences (not her strong point) that were involved in following this path, she decided instead to become a psychiatrist. Because her first love, music, seemed a rather unlikely career to aspire to at that time, psychiatry, or as it later became, social work, made more sense. She remembers, 'I guess it's the thinking bit, trying to communicate with people and help them out. The emotional aspect. It's so sad to see good, nice people emotionally disserved, screwed up when they could be happy.' When her father informed her that she had to become a doctor before she could attempt psychiatric work, she replied that she didn't think she'd need medicine in what she was going to do. Kate says, 'The reason I chose those sort of things is that they are, in a way, the things I do with music. When I write songs I really like to explore the mental area, the emotional values. Although in a way you can say that being a psychiatrist is more purposeful than writing music, in some ways it isn't because a lot of people take a great deal of comfort in music. The really important thing about my music is that all of it is a vehicle for a message.' In an interview with Harry Doherty of *Melody Maker* she quipped, 'I am probably a lot better at being a songwriter than I would be a psychiatrist, for instance. I might have people jumping out of windows by now!'

Music was important to the Bush parents, and they made it an integral part of the upbringing of their children. Kate played the violin at school, although she confesses that it was not through choice. Her father laughingly adds, 'We thought a basic musical grounding would be important. Until she was sixteen, Kate would dutifully give twenty minutes to the violin each day. But not a minute more.' Practice finished, he would hear Kate immediately descend from her room to the piano to commence work on her songs.

Keyboards were always her particular strong point. At an early age she found an old red organ that had belonged to her father in one of the outhouses, and spent most of her time outside teaching herself basic chords. 'I used to play hymns . . . till it was eaten out by mice!' In 1968, when Kate was ten, she 'discovered' the piano. Paddy Bush explains. 'I needed somebody to play the piano to my violin and my father showed her how to play the basic chords and she took it up. She stuck to it, and in her teens, when she felt lonely and frustrated, her music was an outlet.' Kate remembers starting to write when she was about eleven. 'It is something that has gradually progressed into what I am doing now. I think the foundations have been laid from the minute you step out of the womb, from the environment and yourself.' Both Kate's brothers were obsessive about folk music and one of Kate's fondest memories is of them singing Irish and English shanties together.

Dr Bush also used to play and compose on the piano and (although he insists it is just a hobby) began organ lessons at thirty-two, playing at the local church. Kate says, 'When I was very little, my brothers were into traditional folk music, and my father used to play and compose on the piano and I think that was a very strong influence on me. I was very little and there was always music in the house, so it didn't seem unnatural to start playing the piano or playing around on the instruments that were in the house.' Although these early music sessions appear to have been a starting point for Kate's career, her schoolfriends remained unaware of her budding talents. Frances says; 'Although she did play music instruments, strangely enough she never played in the school orchestra, although I believe she supported the school choir.' Kate confirms, 'Actually, when I was in the school choir I couldn't sing the high notes at all. I taught myself as sort of an exercise.' One schoolmate actually likened her to a foghorn!

Kate often spoke of a book she was writing, although to date nothing concrete has ever materialized. She kept her gifts secret from the other girls; she did write poetry, but then so did all her other classmates. Kate notes, 'I used to write poetry like everyone else did in English classes. Everyone was free to read them – we always read each other's work.' A number of Kate's poems found their way into the school magazine. Her lyrical skill is obvious, even at this early age. In the first form she wrote 'The Crucifixion':

He is pushed forward from the steps
Glistening eyes glare from around at the dropping figure
Silence ceases and murmurs gather quickly like the grabbing of a hand
Guilty onlookers hide their eyes from the shame that they know and forbid to
*   reveal*
Slowly the dimness falls.
The man weeps and his forsaken tears fall
Slipping down the trembling and battered body onto the dust.
He collapses down onto the ground.
His head bruises past the stones, scarring his tear-stained face.
He staggers to his feet groping towards his fate.
Sharply, iron pierces flesh, and the stake is raised on the hill.
Stillness overcomes the cheering spectators
And the mocked and pridebroken head turns in outcry.
The people form and run down the hill.
With a last glance at his betrayers,
He dissolves into a limp, dumb body,
As the blood red sun sinks into the skull of a dead man.

Kate Bush was eleven years old when she wrote this. Her descriptive and considerable imagination are evident from other early works, where in fact shreds of the patterns of images that characterize her later work appear in their rudimentary state. Kate was particularly capable in her English classes and consistently won the annual form prize for her well-written compositions and intelligent poetry. Kate's brothers were both highly intellectual and it is easy to imagine that she picked up a number of her ideas and images from their conversation. Her marks in other subjects were no less than average, despite the small amount of time she spent on her studies.

Kate was already writing songs as well as poetry in her early years. 'The Man With The Child In His Eyes' was reputedly written in a very basic form at the age of twelve, which leads to much speculation about the extraordinary insight of this very wise little girl, who had the propensity and the ability to describe and no doubt feel the passions of adult love. Kate confirms, 'From the age of ten I felt old.'

Where Kate's friends were unaware of her musical and lyrical talents, they were also unaware of her ambition to become a musician. Most of her friends were stunned when Kate, formerly regarded as a shy, rather introverted child, displayed the energy, the drive and the discipline to focus her talents so successfully. Kate once explained her reluctance to discuss her aspirations; 'My family and my very close friends knew about it [my music] and that was OK. But I didn't want anyone else to share it. You see, if I had told a boyfriend about my songs he might have thought I was different from the other girls. He might have laughed at me.' Although her sensitivity was not unusual, it was remarkable that her ability to articulate herself had developed to such a degree so early on.

Kate's family were well aware of her abilities. Dr Bush admits that they were all astounded from the first by her natural creative process. 'There's a world of difference between my own plodding compositions and Kate's fusion of gifts. She has "it" and I don't. I think there was some extraordinary spark in her from the start. We simply helped her to get her imagination working. Her songs seemed to write themselves – whole stanzas at a time in her head – while I struggle to put one word after the next. Fragments of her early songs which became hits were already finding their way out of Kate's head by the time she was just thirteen.'

Aside from her unusual gift for music, Kate's childhood was a normal and happy one. She remarks, 'I never went out and beat up old ladies or became an alcoholic at school.' In fact, none of Kate's friends remember her ever being anything other than kind and friendly. The family had a summer home in Birchington near Margate, and when on holiday Kate used to travel on a bus with friends to visit the amusement park nearby. Because Kate's father usually drove her to and fro, a bus ride was a real occasion for young Kate. The summer home in Birchington was a lovely detached house by the sea. The town itself lies on the South-east tip of England, and is inhabited mainly by retired Londoners. It remains elegant and uncommercial.

Kate had a pet rabbit named Took which she allowed to run free in her garden and Wendy house. There is a story told of the time Took's leg was broken by a schoolchum who inadvertently trod upon it. The offending friend was neither chastised nor was Kate obviously angry or alarmed. The rabbit was simply whisked off to the animal hospital without a word. So moved, though, was Kate that she was inspired to write her next poem 'Epitaph For a Rodent'. The rabbit did not, in fact, die, but such was the imagination of a very young, very creative Kate Bush.

Kate doesn't talk a great deal about her early life – that is, the time she spent before leaving school to pursue her music. She had in particular one boyfriend named Alistair Buckle, Alan for short, who was three years older than her. He was five foot ten with sandy hair, and dressed in filthy studded jeans and a leather jacket. Nowadays he works as a civil servant. Kate and her friends would go out to parties and pubs like any other teenagers, the pub most favoured being the 'We Anchor In Hope' not far from her home. In general, though, Kate preferred to remain at home, and the more she got involved in her music, the less she made time for a social life. She remembers, 'Obviously I used to like to go and meet boys, but I mainly just liked playing the piano . . . I was never really into going to discos and dances and stuff.' Frances Byrne relates a story about Kate in her teens: 'During that period of time she was going out with Alastair Buckle, and I was going out with a friend of Alistair's called Martin Montgomery. Both of them were into motorbikes, leather jackets and oily jeans, and I must admit that during the period I tended to dress with the rest in leather and jeans, although Kate was never really a part of that crowd. They used to park their bikes at the pub where we'd all meet now and again for a drink. In fact, Alistair had his twenty-first birthday party there. There is a story told of the day that Kate went looking for him at the "Anchor" but didn't want to come inside, so she left a rose on the petrol tank of his motorbike. That's absolutely true.' Frances remembers Kate as being more a 'flower child in appearance than a ruffian'. Her brothers are also remembered as being 'old age hippies', which accounts for Kate's tendency to dress as she did and to use, to this day, a lot of outdated sixties terms like 'vibes', 'aura', and 'concepts'. Her speech was, and is, often peppered with surreal expletives, which gives the impression that she's not quite 'with us'.

Her brothers certainly had a great influence on Kate. Alan Murphy, a session musician who worked with Kate from her first tour onwards says, 'It seems to me that both Jay and Paddy have been instrumental in . . . not feeding Kate, but supplying her with influences in literature and music and of course, both of them have messed around with all elements of sound and instruments, eastern and western, and so Paddy as an instrumentalist has access to all these things.' Kate worries that the impression the Press have of her brother John is not favourable. 'I'm very close to him. He is an inspiration. Being my brother he is someone I can always talk to . . . what worries me is that sometimes Jay is portrayed as a Svengali who is black and evil. And he's not at all. He's very beautiful and sensitive and I love him very much.'

She used to hold parties in the old barn behind her house, and they are described as being 'large, with an incredible cross-section of people'. One friend remembers being surprised by the kind of friends Kate surrounded herself with because she didn't really seem to fit in with the motorbike crowd. Nonetheless, she began to include her new music friends in her invitations as her circle widened. Kate's family never seemed to mind her parties, although they reputedly grew progressively wilder as her circle expanded.

School who becoming more of a strain for Kate as her songwriting abilities developed. One of Kate's teachers voiced doubts that Kate's musical compositions were her own, and naturally Kate began to find the atmosphere at school, and therefore education in general, stifling. It is likely that there weren't many others at St Joseph's Convent School with her aptitude. Her parents were avid fans of her musical talents, but she was put under some pressure to move on to University to continue her formal education. St Joseph's Convent School proudly claimed that most of their girls progressed to higher education and frowned upon any attempt to give up before A Level.

Kate studied the violin until her mid-teens; her father confirms that she could have been a very good player – if she had kept it up. He explains, 'She just didn't have the interest. Actually, she didn't need to practise'. Her father would accompany her on the piano for her exams, but it was something that came naturally to Kate, and after a few minutes she would know the pieces inside out so that further practice just wasn't necessary. Kate did not have any formal piano training, but her family were aware of her dependence on the piano as an outlet.

The psychological effects of a loving supportive family made their mark on Kate Bush. To this day she credits them with much of her success, taking into account both their encouragement of her music and writing, and their respect for her as a person. As she approached O Levels, however, the frustration, of having no means by which to pursue music as a career was building, and she found herself dispirited by having to continue to work towards an education that she found meaningless. She couldn't possibly have foreseen what was just around the corner.

2

SETTING THE STAGE

You don't need no crystal ball
Don't fall for a magic wand
We humans got it all we perform the miracles
'Them Heavy People'
Kate Bush, 1978

If Kate Bush was becoming increasingly disillusioned with academic life, that was only one of the factors that influenced her decision to leave school and embark upon a career in music.

In 1972, at the tender age of fourteen, Kate was encouraged by her family to present her music in demo form to friend Ricky Hopper, who had some excellent music connections. Although he was impressed with her music – some thirty songs prepared in tape form – he was unsuccessful in placing her music with any of the big recording companies. Her work was described as 'amateurish' and 'morbid'. As she had in the past, Kate again toyed with the idea of social work or psychiatry and took a trip to Newcastle Polytechnic where she stayed for one week and went through the motions of preparing herself for a career in medicine or the like.

Kate's family, however, did not give up on their young protégée and later the same year organized, again through Ricky Hopper, for David Gilmour – a friend of Hopper's from Cambridge University – to listen to Kate's music. Gilmour, of Pink Floyd fame, was instantly convinced of her potential and put up the money for Kate's first professional demo tapes. Kate modestly describes the events: 'I suppose I must have been fifteen, and my family felt it would be interesting to see if we could get some of my songs published. Through a friend of the family [Hopper] we made contact with

13

Dave Gilmour who came and listened. At that time he was scouting for talent, and I think he felt I was sufficiently talented to put up money in order to properly produce three tracks, and through those tracks I got a recording contract.'

It wasn't actually as simple as that. Kate recorded her first demo at Gilmour's home studio, backed by Gilmour on guitar and the Unicorn's bass player and drummer – Pat Martin and Pete Perrier respectively. They chose 'Passing Through Air' and 'Maybe' and the new tape was circulated to the record companies. Kate was still at school studying for her O Levels at this stage, although she admits that she did want to leave and throw herself into music. 'It was what I wanted to do. I didn't want to go to University so I didn't see any point in staying on.' The record companies again turned down her work. The lack of progress was discouraging for Kate, especially as she got so much closer to achieving something through her work with Gilmour. But she continued to write and work on her vocals.

Kate proceeded to take her O Levels and acquired ten passes with excellent results in English, Music and Latin. She continued to take courses for her A Levels although at that point she didn't feel it was very likely that she would go on to the examinations. 'I felt the only reason to stay at school was to take and get exams . . . after O Levels, I felt I just didn't want to go on . . .'.

Gilmour, still intent on getting recognition for Kate, decided that the only course of action that would attract the attention of the record companies would be to prepare a new demo with three songs professionally produced. Enlisting the services of Andrew Powell as producer (noted primarily for his orchestral arrangements and for his work with Alan Parsons) and Geoff Emerick as engineer, Gilmour put up the money for her to prepare the tapes at Air Studios in South-east London. Andrew Powell comments on the first tapes he heard: 'The first songs I was given from her must have contained three or four cassettes with at least sixty songs on, so it was really quite hard to choose, even for the initial demo session. The same thing happened with the first record. I don't know how many songs we sifted through before actually making *The Kick Inside*.' The songs chosen for the maiden demo were 'Man With The Child In His Eyes', 'The Saxophone Song' and 'Maybe'. Gilmour was recording his own album with Pink Floyd – *Wish You Were Here* – at Abbey Road during the following months and he took the opportunity to play the three-track tape for Bob Mercer, then General Manager of EMI's pop division. Mercer was impressed. 'Dave Gilmour asked me to listen to a demo tape with three songs on it, one of which was "The Man With The Child In His Eyes". It was the singer's vocal peculiarity, her range so wide and strong, which really appealed to me.' But that wasn't all. Aside from being astounded by her age – she was only sixteen – he also thought she had 'an unusual talent, something more than her ability to write and perform, a gamine quality that suggests sexual innocence.'

It was shortly after this that EMI made her an offer. Kate recalls: 'It was really exciting for me. It was what I had been hoping for for a few years. It was great. At the same time, it wasn't very easy. You certainly had to fight for what you wanted and I think that's the code for anything. You *do* have to fight for what you want. When you know that there is something that you can aim for, the chances are there will be obstacles you will have to get over in order to get it.'

She had done it. Armed with her ten O Levels and a sizeable inheritance from an aunt who had recently passed away, Kate left school and began her negotiations with EMI. She says, 'The money did enable me to think that I could do it because I was obviously worried about leaving school and finding myself nowhere. I had strong feelings about not having securities like a nice little job. I wanted to try and do what I wanted and if it went wrong, OK, but at least try to do it.' Dr and Mrs Bush were not entirely pleased that she had given up her A Level studies after coming so close to completion, but they too recognized the talent and extraordinary qualities in their daughter. I was overwhelmed when I heard that first tape,' says Dr Bush. 'It was a hell of an achievement and not something gained by practice. You could practise eight hours a day and you wouldn't achieve that.' Her family involved themselves in the negotiation of her contract, as did Gilmour, and Kate was finally signed with a £3000 advance and a four-year contract with options at the end of the second and third years.

It was at about this time that Kate moved out of the family home in Welling and moved into a large house comprising three self-contained flats which she shared with her two brothers. The house was owned by her father, but the layout of separate flats gave her the freedom to be on her own. Home was just half an hour away. The flat was in Brockley, in South-east London, a small suburban district resplendent with old Victorian architecture and plenty of conservation areas. Her flat was minutes from the High Road, where she became a well-known figure, sauntering about in her spare time.

'It's a very ordinary flat, she explained, 'though I like it because it's got all my things in it. It's just far enough out to be nice and quiet. I'd like to live in the country really, but the flat's best for the moment, while I'm working in London, because I can't drive.'

Kate was not called in to record for EMI for another two years, but she was not idle. Considering her age and the fact that she had been handed £3000 – quite a sum for anyone in the late seventies – she was exceedingly mature in the use of her time and in the development of her talents. She spent the time educating herself both physically and vocally. She says, 'I wanted to get some sort of bodily expression together to go with the music. Music is a very emotional thing and there's always a message. Your purpose as a performer is to get it across to the people in as many ways as you can.' It is obvious that Kate had an ideal, a concept of what she wanted to do as a serious performer, even in the early stages. Although she says she had never considered dance at school, she does recall spending time dancing in the privacy of her own room: 'I worked out this dance routine and mime to the Beatles' "Eleanor Rigby". I just lived in the world of the song for days and days, dancing it, getting it right.' Kate comes by her dancing abilities naturally; her mother was a highly accomplished folk dancer in Ireland. Kate's small sinewy body with long slim legs and narrow hips is ideal for dance.

She became particularly attracted to dance when she saw it on stage. Originally Kate had attempted the study of karate but didn't get anywhere with it; her teacher at the time felt she lacked the necessary grace! Kate feels that it was more because she was uninspired by it. Because she had no prior training in dance, she found it difficult to find a placement in a serious dance school and began to direct her efforts towards the study of mime, an art that had always appealed to her. Her first classes were at London's Elephant and Castle under Adam Durius, who is today one of the world's foremost mime artists and runs the self-proclaimed 'only concentrated Mime Centre' at Chalk Farm. Kate had a natural ability and

Durius exclaimed upon her 'remarkable potential'. The classes took place only once a week, leaving Kate strangely unsatisfied.

Several months later, Kate read an advertisement in a London weekly magazine, *Time Out*, that caught her attention, for Lindsay Kemp's *Flowers*, a play choreographed and directed by him. It was this production that had such an impact on Kate. 'The first time I saw him it was like a whole new world opened up for me. He did more than I'd ever seen done on stage before and he never opened his mouth!' *Flowers* must have been slightly shocking to the teenaged Kate, with an opening scene that portrayed several characters masturbating on the set. She was, however, enchanted by the production and claims it was one of the great inspirations to her as a performer. 'Once I'd seen *Flowers* I knew I had to do something which would be my own *Flowers* – not necessarily a show'. The rather unorthodox but highly acclaimed Kemp was one of the great influences on Bowie in his *Ziggy Stardust* and 'Young American' days. He described his classes as aimed at those who wish to live fabulously through their senses, and offered a rounded course-structure of dance, pantomime and vocals. Kate began to attend his classes at a dance centre in Covent Garden.

Kate describes it thus: 'It was through seeing a show that Lindsay Kemp did that I thought dance would be an extremely useful way of expressing myself besides music, and if I wanted to be a performer, that would help me a lot. When I left school, I started training as a dancer and working on my music on a full time basis. I joined the dance class as one of the students and really only trained with him for two or three months before he went to Australia. From then on I got lessons when I could but went into a more straight form of dance, learning contemporary dance, and touched on ballet and just tried different things.

Lindsay Kemp remembers Kate well. 'I met Kate Bush, like I meet many people, like so many of my friends, like I met all my company, and that was in classes – classes at the Dance Centre. The classes were very very large, and I think that by the time she spoke to me – she was terribly nervous – it was one tea break and she explained that she'd already had about a dozen classes with me, and I must say I hadn't noticed her at all. The classes were large and she was the type of girl, child almost, that stayed at the back. After that I began to notice her more – when we'd had a chat and so on. I saw this tiny shining thing. She reminded me of Tinkerbell or Wendy or something.'

Kate Bush was often likened to a child not only for her vocals in songs like 'The Man With The Child In His Eyes' but also because of her size and demeanour. In her later years she expended a great deal of energy trying to refute this image, exclaiming crossly, 'I am not an elf, I am a woman'. She went so far, however, as to place herself on the verge of a 'tits and ass' image, which she had to spend another energetic session trying to avoid. Perhaps Kemp hit the nail on the head by calling her a Wendy or a Tinkerbell. She does in fact vocalize this very ideal in 'In Search Of Peter Pan' on the *Lionheart* album.

Kemp was obviously very impressed by Kate. 'She gave everything in class. From that tiny, frail, shy person came this fabulous amount of drama. She loved the drama, you know. And later on, I gave her a job in my wardrobe. I realized that she was extremely talented. I didn't like to take her money. I offered her a job in the wardrobe at The Roundhouse, helping make the costumes for *Mr Punch* which was preparing at the time, in return for free classes. She probably didn't need free classes because I think her family was quite well off, and I learned later that she was under contract to EMI, and one of the reasons that she was studying with me was part of her grooming programme. She was already being groomed for stardom and she never let on. She has always been marvellously humble.' Lindsay Kemp goes on in all humility himself, 'I only helped her a little bit. I didn't give her the talent, you know. I didn't give her the passion for work. I didn't give her the energy. I just helped her a bit to dance, to be a little louder than before.'

Dance and mime were to become very important in the Kate Bush phenomenon and to her ideal that a performance should involve more than simply vocals. She continued to work on her music, training her voice to reach its incredible heights. She bought herself a £200 honkytonk piano and worked on the songs she had prepared previously, adding several new ones to her repertoire. She wrote a letter to schoolfriend Francis Byrne at about this time which indicates that her expansion into the realms of those being groomed for stardom had not affected her character in the least:

Dear Fran,

Thanks for your letter – it was really, really nice to hear from you, but not a total surprise – it was strange because you appeared for a split second in my dream last night and your letter was at my parents' this morning. It's good to hear you're so well and coping with your life – Well Done – it gets really hard sometimes, dun it?

I gather you hear I've left school? Well, I left during last year's summer holidays – before they all went back for the Autumn Term. I've only been back once since, and that was an extremely brief visit, but that's how it goes . . . ! I now go to an open dance college in London. It's called the Dance Centre, and it's OK. It is expensive and my life is, at the moment, revolving around the money that's left over from the lessons, but that's enough for me to have fun and buy cigarettes. (I am afraid to say that I'm smoking quite a lot but I think I've got it under control?) I haven't heard from you for so long that it's difficult to know where to start. I guess you know that I have set myself a definite ambition as a career. I want to sing, write songs and mime. I've got a contract actually being drawn up by a record company at last, but it has taken 4 years (approximately) to get this far – but I think it is going to get more progressive – I hope so. I'm working quite hard on my voice and on songs (and dancing too I suppose) but I seem to spend most of time time waiting for it all to happen. Last summer I took mime lessons with Lindsay Kemp. He is an amazing person and I met a lot of nice friends through the classes. The more people I meet now, the older and stranger they seem to get – it's funny . . . I've had my two front teeth straightened at the dentist. The appointment was 2½ hours long and he's put temporary crowns in at the moment, but they're nice – it's just that I'm a bit paranoid about the fact that they're held in by glue – I really hope they don't fall out! I also failed my driving test in March, but I'll take it again in August. I've got your phone number. It would be really nice to see you again . . . one night, for old times' sake, huh? I'm in Lewisham now in a very beautiful flat, above my brothers – I'm very free and very happy. Anyway, Fran, I'll give you a ring in the next month or two (I say that far away because I know how inefficient I am at getting things like that together, but this, I will, eventually, honest).

Lots of Love

Kate.

PS No, I don't really see people from school much, but I find it so strange when I do – I feel so, so, different, very far away from them.

The letter gives a good idea of Kate's honesty, humility and her

19

characteristic 'niceness'. She continued to make time for old friends all the way through her career, one of the reasons why there are truly very few people with anything unkind to say about her.

Two months later, inspired by seeing the BBC film presentation of *Wuthering Heights*, Kate wrote her most successful song to date – reputedly in August of 1977 under a full moon, and called it 'Wuthering Heights'. Aside from the theatrics involved with the event, the song is certainly a tribute to both her originality as a songwriter and the strength and unusual range of her voice. Describing the vocals of the song, Kate says: 'I really try to project myself into the role of Cathy and so, as she is a ghost, I give her a high-pitched wailing voice . . . the imagery there was so strong, where two people were so in love, not necessarily in a healthy way; in a very possessive way. It is really all about possession. The whole thing of Cathy dying and not leaving him alone – she'd come back to get him and there's no way they can be parted – she's just this totally possessive spirit. I think at that time I was trying to tell the story and create the sense of a spirit coming back to take a human. But it is all about passion really, and possessive love.' Kate did go on to read the book, which she described as 'incredible'. A number of the songs that Kate wrote in her Brockley flat were in fact love songs, including a number of extremely sensuous ones such as 'Feel It' and 'L'Amour Looks Something Like You', which appeared on her first album.

By this time Kate had ended things with Alistair and started up with Del Palmer, an artist and bass-player friend of her brother Paddy's. She is with him today. Not long after their first union, they moved in together. It has been suggested that the elder Bushes were not enamoured with Del Palmer, but it appears that he has added a great deal to her creative process over the years, especially on albums like *The Dreaming* where his bass and drums are so significant. They met sometime in her childhood but worked together for the first time in April 1977 when Kate and her brother put together the KT Band. It was only about three or four months before the first album. She says, 'Some friends of my brother were putting a band together and wanted a lead singer, and I thought it was just a perfect opportunity to get some experience and see what it was like. It was a lot of fun, but as I said, we only did it for about three or four months and then I was in to make the first album. We did clubs and just any places we could get gigs in the area. It was very good and it was lots of fun!'

The band members included Del Palmer, Paddy Bush, Brian Bath and Charlie Morgan, and their first gig took place at the Rose of Lee pub in Lewisham. Frances Byrne remembers, 'At the time we lost touch, I remember some friends saying that Kate was playing with a band down at a pub called the Rose of Lee, which is just outside Lewisham in Lee Green. It's one of those rough sort of pubs in which a salubrious section doesn't really exist, but I suppose looking back on it, that must have been her first live performance.' The band played predominantly rock and roll numbers, including covers of 'Honky Tonk Woman', 'Satisfaction' and 'Come Together'. Kate tried out a few of her own songs and they were greeted with an enthusiastic response. Later, on a BBC presentation, Kate described one rather disconcerting gig appearance: 'We were in Putney on the eve of the football match between Scotland and England and all these Scottish guys were in there and they were mad, they were just mad. They had flags waving everywhere, and no-one could see the stage because all the guys were getting up on stage and putting their arms around you, and it was a bit hard to keep singing when everyone was poking sticks in your eyes. But they were good, they were good people.'

The experience was not enough to discourage Kate, and she continued playing until just a few months later when she was called in by EMI. They were ready. And so was she.

3
DEBUT

But who's to know the power
Behind our moves
'Strange Phenomena'
Kate Bush, 1978

In a move of extraordinary foresight, EMI chose to give Kate Bush nearly two years in which to develop and cultivate her talents, as opposed to exploiting her fresh-faced originality immediately. In the years before she recorded *The Kick Inside*, Kate had become a master of her art as well as enhancing it with the dance and mime techniques she had fostered as a part of her growth. In August 1977 EMI made the arrangements for Kate to record her first album, calling upon Andrew Powell, who was responsible for the production of her first three songs on the initial demo tape, to produce. Jon Kelly was to engineer. Work began immediately at Air Studios in London, with backing by members of the pop groups Cockney Rebel and Pilot.

With the help of Andrew Powell, Kate made the selection of tracks for the album, choosing 'The Man With The Child In His Eyes' and 'The Saxophone Song' from her earlier work for EMI. Jon Kelly remembers the selection process: 'I think his [Andrew Powell's] influence was that he chose the material from Kate's huge catalogue. She had so many songs she'd been writing over the years before she made her frist record – I think she's been writing from the age of twelve or thirteen. She had so many songs to choose from and Andrew just had to choose. His influence on the material was a big one, I think, in the material he chose for that first album.'

23

Andrew Powell himself was astonished at the number of songs from which to choose and the quality of each. He says, 'It was very difficult . . . there were several songs that were obviously very good that didn't end up on the first album. One or two of them were used on the second album. She didn't have a clear idea of what she wanted to do at first because she'd literally hardly ever been in a recording studio – certainly not a professional studio.'

Kate picked up the procedures almost immediately, and with her characteristic optimism and ambition started using the studio as another instrument with which to enhance her music. Andrew Powell remembers thinking that it was odd for someone so young to be so creative in both her own development and the use of the equipment and stimuli that surrounded her. 'There was a period in between recording the initial tracks, as I say two of which ended up on the record *The Kick Inside*, and actually recording the main body of the record – maybe eighteen months or so. I think a lot of people would have become very depressed in that period and sort of negative; but she kept on writing and she decided that she wanted to start learning to dance and get certain visual aspects of what would eventually be her stage or video act together. She went and studied mime and went to dance classes and used the time in a very creative way rather than sitting around wondering why it wasn't happening. She's really quite a bright girl, and she picked up all sorts of ideas very quickly indeed as to what you could do and how to start using the studio as something rather than being subjugated by it. She learnt very quickly how to use it for a tool to her own end.'

The final selection for *The Kick Inside* included thirteen songs, all her own, many of which she had written in her early teenage years. *The Kick Inside* remains even now one of Kate Bush's critically most acclaimed albums, commended for its incredibly unusual voice patterns. The album was a showcase for Kate's voice, and she swoops and trills her way through a variety of what could otherwise be considered naïve and unspectacular love songs. The album has a distinct 60s flavour to it; in a year when ABBA and Blondie were the supremos of the music charts, Kate Bush was an oddity both in sound and in lyric.

Used to being entirely the master of her own work, Kate had to settle for simple piano arrangements and piano playing alongside her vocals on this first album. It is, however, the only album on which she allowed the control of her music to slip to anyone else to any degree. Andrew Powell's orchestrative talents are evident; in fact a number of the songs on that first album were done live with orchestras. Jon Kelly remembers that although Kate had a premeditated idea of what she wanted to do in the studio, she was quite happy to sit back and let Powell take over as she soaked in the recording processes. He says, 'I could see that she was going to develop. She does love the studio. It was really where she wanted to be and it was her vocation to be in the studio recording and using her songs and mapping out the ideas she had for arrangements and the material. She was always extremely accommodating and accepted criticism very readily.'

It was an entirely new experience for Kate Bush; however, her speed in assimilating recording technique was a surprise to the technicians. Because creative people with an unusual and highly stylistic output tend to be more difficult, it was refreshing for them to find Kate Bush intensely interested in the opinions of those who surrounded her. Powell notes: 'I have very fond memories, particularly, of that first record. it was one of the most enjoyable records I've worked on, partly because it was done so quickly. It only took six or seven weeks of actual studio time, which is really very fast, and that helped immensely. Sometimes you have to listen to ten songs for six months – it can even be two years in some cases.'

For an amateur, Kate was extremely adept in the initial presentation of her work. Her lyrics were always presented in virtually finished form. Powell remembers a couple of incidents where maybe one or two words were slightly changed, but in general the manner in which it was presented as a demo would be the way it ended up on the record itself. He says, 'I can think of very few other artists I have worked with where we haven't changed a word or even, as far as I can remember, a single chord on most of the songs. Most of the songs are on record as they were initially written, which is very unusual.' He also remembers her being very easy to work with. 'On the first album it was easier because she knew relatively little about what was going on, she would listen far more and take direction.'

Jon Kelly remembers meeting Kate early on. 'She was very young and very quiet and very very naïve. I was impressed by her songs. The first day working with her we recorded three songs called "Moving", "L'Amour Looks Something Like You" and "Wuthering Heights", which we did all in the first day. We did the backing tracks for them and I was most impressed. I couldn't believe the quality of the songs, and she actually sat down at the piano and played them all live with the group. There were four other musicians, drums, bass, guitar and organ, as I remember. The tracks were virtually put down live. It was a fantastic experience because there was so much atmosphere in the way she sang and performed. The sounds of Kate's records come from the way she writes her songs and the way she performs them. That's the way she makes a Kate Bush record sound the way it does. It's because *she's* written it and *she's* singing it and the arrangement that works for the song is the one that works best with her material. The sound isn't something that you can premeditate. You don't think about making the sound of a record before you've actually heard it or recorded it. The way it is recorded is the way it sounds.'

The production of the album became a living and breathing project for Kate Bush, and Kelly remembers thinking that she would have been pleased to stay in the studio for twenty-four hours a day. However, a typical recording day began sometime after noon, usually closer to two in the afternoon, running until eight or nine in the evening, although that wasn't where the day ended for Kate. She worked continuously, usually into the small hours of the morning, to 'get it right'. The perfecting of her voice and the backing vocals became a near obsession. She was indeed exemplary in doing most of her own backing vocals, which she did partly because there was difficulty in finding vocalists with the extended ranges she had accomplished; further, it became part of the process for her, part of the development of a 'Kate Bush production', that the whole album should be very much Kate Bush inspired and contrived. Powell remarks, 'One thing right from the start that interested me was that Kate would initially give the songs to me in a demo form with just herself playing piano and singing, and we would then record a backing track with drums, bass guitar, her playing piano and additional keyboards, and obviously move on to another song. She would take a mix of this home and start working out ideas of what she wanted to do with backing vocals, and come in with sometimes four parts, sometimes sixteen or seventeen different parts that would all dovetail and fit into each other – really quite well orchestrated. Right from the start she was very interested in the possibilities of different sounds from her voice and how she could use extreme ranges and that sort of thing.' Kate claims that her voice is not forced to such extremities. She admits to cultivating various sounds, unusual or otherwise, but the range and the extraordinary timbre are natural: 'Honestly, I opened my mouth and that's what came out.'

Despite the inevitable clashes that occurred when both Powell and Bush dug in their heels over particular tracks, it was an amicable and productive union. Members of the backing bands remember it being a 'family' sort of unit – friendly, helpful and unassuming.

It was only September by the time the album was completed, and in an uncharacteristic move EMI bowed to Kate's request to release 'Wuthering Heights' first in lieu of their choice, 'James And The Cold Gun'. It was quite a risk to go with 'Wuthering Heights', a strange song that could well have labelled Kate as a one-hit wonder. The track was freakish, with her dramatic falsetto screeching its way through the highly imaginative rendition of Emily Brontë's classic novel. In a number of cases, the song was actually looked upon as a disservice to her abilities because of the exaggerated nature of the vocals. As a result of its bizarre originality, however, Kate immediately gained recognition and more than a handful of firm fans. As a song it was a tough act to follow, and it was only thanks to the strength of the remainder of the very different songs on *The Kick Inside* that she was able to establish fully her credibility both as a singer and songwriter.

The other tracks on the album which confirm her mastery of the ballad form are 'The Man With The Child In His Eyes', 'Moving' and 'L'Amour Looks Something Like You'. In the same genre, there is the eerie sound of 'The Kick Inside' in which she verges on excellence as she quietly and hauntingly tells of the departure from an incestuous union: *'This kicking here inside makes me leave you behind/No more under the quilt to keep you warm/Your sister I was born – you must lose me'*. The song is reputedly based on the ballad 'Lucy Wan' which portrays an incestuous relationship between brother and sister. In the ballad, brother murders sister when he finds her pregnant with his child. In Kate's version she makes an imaginative play on the folk music influence that infiltrated the Bush psyche so firmly. It is a poignant and melodic number, subtly probing the feelings of incest and an inevitable need to commit suicide. There is a resigned, whimsical tone to the song and it ends abruptly in mid-verse.

In 'James And The Cold Gun', a more contemporary upbeat number, she admonishes James of the James Gang outlaws and makes clear that she can 'rock' with the best of them. No doubt EMI had chosen this as their ideal first single for that very reason. Kate Bush is obviously well aware of her sexuality. And then in contrast to the very innocent 'The Man With The Child In His Eyes', there is 'Feel It' in which she manages to titillate the senses with her erotic cry: *'Oh I need it oh oh feel it feel it my love/. . . See what you're doing to me'.* And similarly, in 'L'Amour Looks Something Like You', she discusses the *'feeling of sticky love inside'*, hot stuff for EMI's protégée of 'nice girl' rock. It's easy to see where she picked up her following of hardcore male fans!

'Moving' begins with the sounds of whale cries, or 'singing', a stylistic detail which Jon Kelly assures was entirely Kate's own inspiration. 'Moving' was allegedly written for Lindsay Kemp, who inspired her to find satisfaction and a completion of her art through movement. 'The Saxophone Song' is reminiscent of the 50s German jazz singles, with Alan Skidmore capably accompanying on the saxophone. Her voice is deeper and stronger in this one, refusing to rollercoaster the scales as normal. The lyrics reflect a complex imagery that is developed more fully in some of her later work ('Violin' for instance): the song sees the narrator alone in a Berlin bar, fighting an obsession for the seductive music of the saxophone. She croons, *'You'll never know that you had all of me/. . . There's something very real in how I feel honey.'*

'Strange Phenomena' takes us back to the usual exploitation of her vocal range, taking a look a premonition and mystical experience in everyday life. Bush is known for her belief in 'other powers', commenting most sincerely in an interview with an astonished *Melody Maker* journalist that she may well have met him in another life. In any case, 'Strange Phenomena' is convincing, and with the

'Cathyesque' shrieking associated with 'Wuthering Heights' incorporated, it is a track that could well have been released as a single and fared well.

'Them Heavy People' is a tribute to the influences of Gilmour and Kemp, as her album dedication confirms: 'Much thanks and love to Dave Gilmour for rolling the ball in the beginning', and thanks to 'my teachers of music and movement for being heavy'. One can't help but think that her brothers are also included in the acknowledgements because of her references in the song 'They Read Me' to 'Gurdjieff and Jesu', and 'I must work on my mind'. Kate has often admitted that her brothers were responsible for much of her intellectual development and thus bore a great influence on her lyrics which, on a number of occasions, border on being literary as well as musical feats.

The remainder of the album includes 'Kite', 'Room For The Life' – a song that gained her a great deal of praise in feminist circles – and 'Oh To Be In Love', in which she lashes out against one-night stands and longs for the comfort of one love. It was an extraordinary first album, and illustrates clearly the range of vocalistic techniques that she had cultivated.

It was 4th November of the same year, 1977, that EMI set as the date for the release of her first single, 'Wuthering Heights'. In a flash of artistic integrity, Kate persuaded EMI to change the sleeve of the album from the very flattering but rather sexist photograph of her clad in a pink, very tight, top to the photographic extravaganza which constituted Del Palmer's visual impression of the song 'Kite'. The alteration necessitated changes in all the previously prepared promotional material, and by the time EMI had organized the new campaign, it was nearly Christmas, the period of millions and mayhem for record companies. Uneasy with launching a new artist into this situation, EMI delayed the release of the single until January the following year.

Because of the necessary prepromotion associated with first time artists, EMI had already sent a number of demos out to the network of radio stations and experienced trouble retrieving them. This proved to be most fortunate for Kate as Capital Radio, one of London's foremost commercial radio stations, latched onto the song with a fury. It is generally claimed that they are responsible for the initial rise of 'Kate Bush Fever'. Tony Myatt, successful DJ for the station, remembers: 'I was doing a late night programme for Capital Radio and my producer at the time was a guy called Eddie Puma. Eddie used to find unusual things to play on the programme and one night I saw on my script, 'Kate Bush – "Wuthering Heights". I'd seen the actual sleeve cover of the single which I thought was very nice and he said, "Have a listen and tell me what you think of this." He made some other comment about it, something like "he liked it" or "it was a strange record", so when I played it my first reaction was "My God, I've never heard anything like this". So I put a little note on the script, "Very impressed, we must play more – lots". And that's when it started. I think we were the very first people to play that record by Kate, and from that point on eveything seemed to snowball for her. People were calling up and saying "What was that unbelievable record?"

The demand for the single soared and because Eddie Puma and Tony Myatt were so convinced that it was a big record, the other stations began to catch on. Myatt says, 'I think after that a lot of the other stations like, for example, Radio 1 – I don't think they were playing the record initially – started to play it, and Kate became very talked about'.

In January the following year, 1978, Kate attended a three-day international sales conference for EMI and, after singing live, was hailed as the new superstar in the EMI stable. On the 20th of the same month, 'Wuthering Heights' was officially released and after only two weeks rose to number 42 in the charts. From here, the whirlwind of Kate Bush's career took off, and in the next month she made a TV appearance in an abandoned Railway Station in Germany for the highly acclaimed 'Bio's Banhof' on WDR TV. The scenery supplied by the station for 'Wuthering Heights' included a volcano which was obviously their impression of the moors. Kate recalls: 'I guess that's what they thought an English moor looked like . . . they had a hard time believing we really don't have volcanoes in England!'

In late January, Kate Bush did her first live interview with Tony Myatt. He recalls, 'I'd never met her, and Eddie asked whether I'd like to do an interview with Kate Bush. I said I would love to, and so she came in. I think she was nineteen years old at the time – she was very young, anyway, in her teens – and a lovely guy from EMI called Malcolm Hill brought her in for the interview. The first thing that struck me about Kate was that she looked so young and so pretty, and when we started talking – I mean, this girl is so intelligent it's just ridiculous. I think probably because she reads an awful lot. It was a very intelligent conversation. She was so easy and nice to talk to, and of course I couldn't take my eyes off her because she is so beautiful . . . I think the combination of having all that beauty and all that talent is unbelievable in one person. We did the interview, which we broadcast, and from that moment on everything, as I said, started to snowball for her. She was doing more interviews. Everybody wanted to talk to Kate Bush. The television programmes wanted her – her career just took off from that moment onwards and she's never looked back.'

During her absence in Germany, the single leaped to number 27 and she returned to make her debut performance on British Television on 'Top Of The Pops'. Clad in black top, red trousers and black stiletto heels, she made an instant impression. She was displeased with it herself, and later commented, 'It was like watching myself die'.

Melody Maker quickly caught on to the Kate Bush phenomenon, and Ian Birch wrote, 'Bizarre, Kate is a complete newcomer, is nineteen, was first unearthed by David Gilmour and has spent time with mime coach to the stars, Lindsay Kemp . . . The theatre influence comes through strongly from the cover . . . to every aspect of Kate's song. The orchestration is ornate and densely packed, but never overflows its banks, Kate's extraordinary vocals skating in and out, over and above. Reference points are tricky, but possibly a cross between Linda Lewis and Macbeth's three witches is closest. She turns the famous examination text by Emily Brontë into a glorious soap opera trauma . . .'

The stage was set. Over the next month, Kate performed live on a number of UK television shows, including 'Saturday Night At The Mill'. When the single moved to number 5 in the British charts, Kate Bush joined the realms of the most photographed women in the world, and with confidence building she prepared her first video for 'Wuthering Heights'. The initial video, directed by Keef Macmillan of Debbie Harry fame, had Kate cartwheeling in a flimsy white night dress across the moors. Another video for the track was also made, featuring Kate in a leotard on a stage made foggy with dry ice. It was this video that was chosen for UK use, although the former found its way into the USA and Canada, where it was received with mixed reactions.

On 7 March 1978, Kate Bush went to number 1 in the charts, knocking supergroup ABBA from their exalted position at the helm, much to the glee of the popular music Press. The *Daily Express* called her 'Wuthering Wonderful'; and 'A Tonic for the Doctor's Daughter!' cried the *Daily Mirror*. EMI lavished a champagne reception on her to celebrate the feat, and she was flown off to Paris for a congratulatory dinner. Kate treated herself by replacing her old honkytonk piano with a Steinway baby-grand costing nearly £7,000, and as if in reaction to this, the single went silver.

So Kate Bush was in more ways than one the woman of the year on the pop scene. If you didn't actually hear her music, you couldn't help but notice her staring down from billboards and the sides of double-decker buses. Featured in a pink leotard with ample bust peeking out and over, and all the innocence she could muster she caught the attention of anyone gifted with the faculty of sight. Powell discusses her obviously sensual appearance: 'I think she objected to the sexual image of those early sessions. When they were done, perhaps at the time she wasn't quite aware of it. She'd be asked "just one quick last shot – do it for us", and having done a whole session of very serious pictures, she'd suddenly do something a little bit silly, and that of course would be the one they'd use.' Kate felt confident, however, that she was not taking advantage of her appearance and obvious sexuality – 'I suppose the poster is reasonably sexy just because you can see my tits, but I think the vibes from the face are there.'

Kate Bush had taken the music world by storm, and at the age of only nineteen had established herself as the primo star of the EMI list. 'Wuthering Heights' remained at number 1 for four weeks, and after a second performance on 'Top of the Pops' Kate began a series of live interviews in Ireland and England, including one on BBC TV's current affairs programme, 'Tonight'.

At the end of March 1978, *The Kick Inside* was released in the USA

32

to a disappointing reaction. To the surprise and chagrin of EMI, Kate failed to make an impression. America ostensibly found her 'too unusual', which contradicts rather harshly the stereotypical 'open-minded' American ideal. *The Kick Inside* was released with a different sleeve in America than in the UK, but later American pressings featured the UK cover design, probably because of the much more enthusiastic response her album had received in the UK. She wasn't, it seemed, set to crack the American market for another three or four years.

'Wuthering Heights' moved down to the number 3 spot in the UK at the same time that *The Kick Inside* peaked. With no sign of her energy flagging, Kate set off for Europe – to the Netherlands, West Germany and France – to promote the album. In Amsterdam she filmed a 25-minute, 7-single promotional video at Die Eftelung, a horror/amusement park. Moving on to Germany, she appeared on 'Scene 78' with the Boomtown Rats, her first meeting with lead singer Bob Geldof with whom she was later to share the 1979 *Melody Maker* readers' poll Awards. Next, Kate made her first promotional trips to Canada and the USA, the former greeting her with a tremendous fanfare in sharp contrast to the USA reaction.

While she was promoting abroad, 'Wuthering Heights' went gold in the UK, having sold 500,000 copies. A beaming Kate Bush presented the disc to Tony Myatt at Capital Radio where it hung in the lobby for over four years. Jon Kelly recalls her success: 'Once you'd heard one of Kate's songs, you just couldn't forget it whether you liked it or hated it. You could tell from the moment she walked into the studio on that first day of recording. I was sure she was going to be very successful but I had no idea how successful. It was immediate. I think the radios played it – Capital Radio people worked very hard on it – and it picked up. I'm sure she must have been surprised by it all – the first record you make at the age of nineteen goes to number 1 within six or eight weeks from the day of release. It was tremendous.'

As 'Wuthering Heights' moved its way back out of the charts, Kate chose, with EMI's approval, 'The Man With The Child In His Eyes' as the second single. The song had always been a particular favourite of both Kate's and Dave Gilmour's, and was one that had been recorded during the 1975 session at Gilmour's expense. It was an immediate success. It's an odd song, in the sense that Bush wrote it in her pre-teens, a fact that lead to much discussion at the time. What was a young girl who had so much insight into a man at that age up to? And who was it that visited her bedroom so late at night: '*And when I stay up late/He's always waiting.*'? Kate explains her view of the song: '[It] is very much about how men are very like children, and it was talking about a man who could still take delight in the innocence of things; the idea of an adult not really having grown old but still very much being a child. I think that is something that is more constant in men. I think there are a lot of men who don't grow up. I don't think anyone really grows up, but in some men . . . I think it's a positive thing to sometimes not let go of that. It was just an observation and at the time I liked the line; I liked the idea of the innocence of a person shining in their eyes'. Those were pretty astute observations for a twelve- or thirteen-year-old.

Riding hot on the heels of 'Wuthering Heights', there was much scepticism about whether 'The Man With The Child In His Eyes' could match the success of its predecessor. Tony Myatt explains: 'With the tremendous success of "Wuthering Heights" I can remember thinking at the time how difficult it would be to follow the success of that single, but with the release of "The Man With The Child In His Eyes" (which must be one of my all time favourites) I can remember the album *The Kick Inside* was just starting to move down the charts, but when that single was released the album started moving back up.'

Kate felt very strongly that 'The Man With The Child In His Eyes' should be released as her follow-up single. In an interview with Harry Doherty of *Melody Maker* she said, 'I so want "The Man With The Child In His Eyes" to do well. I'd like people to listen to it as a songwriting song, as opposed to something weird, which was the reaction to "Wuthering Heights". If the next song had been similar straight away I would have been labelled, and that's something I really don't want. As soon as you've got a label, you don't do anything!'

With another hit under her belt, Kate began to make plans for a tour scheduled to take place at the end of the year. Before the itinerary could be set, however, Kate was whisked off to Japan for the 7th Tokyo Song Festival. Choosing 'Moving' as her Japanese debut, she came third in the contest while the single was sent fluttering up the Japanese charts to number 1. Within three months, the little lady with the big voice was well on her way to international acclaim, and before she could sit back and properly enjoy it, EMI were knocking on her door for album number two. 'Imagine,' said Kate graciously when asked about her success, 'and I've only just begun.'

4
OVATION

How did I come to be here anyway?
It's terribly vague what's gone before
I could have been anyone.
                    'Oh To Be In Love'
                    Kate Bush, 1978

Kate was required to come up with the material for her second album *Lionheart* in under four weeks. Annoyed by the pressure EMI were putting on her, she stated that she felt her creativity was being stifled. Nonetheless, in a rudimentary studio – which would, at a later date develop into the fully equipped studio where she works today – designed by her brother Paddy and built with money earned from *The Kick Inside*, Kate produced the demo for the new album. Only three new songs were written in the alotted four weeks; the others that appeared on the album were revamped renditions of her older work.

The successful team of Andrew Powell and Jon Kelly were recruited to work on the second album and Kate herself took a much livelier role in the actual recording and mixing. This was the last album that Powell would produce and Kate was credited as assisting with the production of *Lionheart*. Jon Kelly remembers the pressure that Kate was under to complete the new tracks: 'The record company was expecting her to rush around all over the place both in England doing radio interviews and promotion and travelling all around Europe and America. We went to Japan at one point to do some promotion together as well. You suddenly find that from being a fairly free individual, sitting at home, writing your songs, you're working eighteen hour days virtually in a business, and that presents

37

another problem, because suddenly, after a certain number of months, the record company say, "Its time for a new record – we hope you've written ten good new songs". Of course, it's very hard to find time to write songs when you're doing nothing but getting on and off planes and jostling around airports, running in and out of hotels and radio stations and Press conferences.' Kate acknowledged the same problems: 'The creative process is so alien to the promotional process. Really I learned very quickly after the first single that if I wasn't careful, I could spend twice as much time promoting than actually doing the thing that I was promoting, which is the album or whatever. At that stage, I decided it had to be turned around . . . promotion is very important, but if you're not careful, it leaves you shell-shocked and takes you further away from your creative processes. It's that much harder to get back and it is very time consuming. I find I do have to spend time getting the feel for being creative and playing with ideas and things.'

The pressures that EMI applied were heightened by the fact that Kate was no longer free to walk around at her leisure for fear of being recognized. It was a strain to attempt to produce a creative and original second album to follow an incredible first success. There were still sceptics in the industry who felt her first album was a fluke, that she was a one-album artist, that EMI had dredged her up because of her originality, just to make a bit of money. She was, by all definitions, famous, and for the first quarter of 1978 was the bestselling female album artist in the UK. 'Wuthering Heights' was in the number 1 position all over Europe, including Denmark, Sweden and Finland as well as Brazil, Australia and South Africa. Even if it was her own, it was quite an act to follow.

The crew for the album convened at Superbear Studios in Nice, where the lovely weather revitalized an exhausted Kate. Dave Gilmour had recommended this studio as it was here that he had recorded his first solo album. The strain of the recording process was alleviated to a certain degree by the pleasant surroundings, and Kate was able to come up with twelve tracks, ten of which appear on the album. The recording took only ten weeks.

For the first time, Kate came into some conflict with Andrew Powell. He says, 'On the first album it was much easier because she knew relatively little about what was going on, she would listen far more and take direction, but by the time we got to the second record she had learnt a lot more about what she wanted, and inevitably it did conflict with what I wanted, at times, and what I thought about things. There were disagreements. That's bound to happen if you've got several creative people working together in the same room on something. There are not that many art forms – I suppose theatre, opera or whatever – where you have a committee of people as it were – an artist, a producer, an engineer, and quite often a record company executive, all involved in what's going to happen. If someone is painting a picture, it's not that often that he gets someone to tell him what to do.'

Powell does not harbour any resentment or harsh feelings about being ousted from his position as her sole producer. Any clashes of ideas, he assures, were sorted out fairly amicably. 'We would sometimes try something her way, sometimes my way. Whichever way sounded better was what would end up happening.'

Kate did have much more to say on the album, feeling that where *The Kick Inside* was aimed at the senses, *Lionheart* was aimed at the guts. It turned out to be far less surreal, lyrically, and the theme of the 'fantastic' quality of dreams, phantoms and old ballads was less prominent. *Lionheart* deals with the concrete, with reality. Two of her songs deal with homosexuality, another is a tribute to her country, and several deal quite explicitly with the joys of sex. To suggest that they are not imaginative would be a mistake, for Kate Bush has never lost any of her extraordinarily fertile imagination. This album seems, rather, to be more analytical, more in touch with gut feelings than external sensations.

Kate insisted, against Andrew Powell's advice, on using her own KT Band on a number of the tracks. It is generally agreed that the band, replete with unusual talents (such as Paddy Bush on the Mandolin), did contribute heavily to the success of the album. Feeling concerned that *The Kick Inside* had her labelled as 'ethereal' and 'soft', she took steps to create a harsher, more professional impression of herself. Her lyrics are much stronger, based on more, concrete subject matter and her vocals, although this is difficult to imagine, are more controlled, depending less on the exotic rushes up and down the scales: they are much more theatrical, more practised and kept within more rigid confines.

The unashamed sexuality of Kate Bush which became apparent on the first album is alive and thriving on this one. Side One begins with a strong number, 'Symphony In Blue', characterized by Del Palmer's heavy bass. Lines like *'The more I think about sex/The better it gets'* don't leave much to the imagination and she is equally explicit in 'In The Warm Room': *'She'll let you watch her undress/Go places where your fingers long to linger . . . Say hello to the soft musk of her hollows.'* The song relies heavily on the ballad technique that was used so successfully on the first album, but is rather less spectacular in the sense that there are not the unresolved contradictions that characterized 'The Kick Inside' and 'The Man With The Child In His Eyes'.

'Oh England My Lionheart' takes the form of a traditional ballad, with all care taken to control its medieval sound. Harpsicord, mandolin and the rest of the Paddy Bush influence create a surprisingly intense and authentic track, considering patriotic numbers tend to be regarded as bland. Paddy was influential in helping Kate locate 'just the right sound' she was looking for. His vast collection and knowledge of unusual instruments has always complemented Kate's music. Simon Drake, the illusionist on her tour, comments: 'Paddy did a hell of a lot of backing vocals, and he's an incredible character – always very interested in everything, very hungry for knowledge, and he's got a really good sense of humour – a very nice guy. In his flat there were musical instruments adorning the walls. That's his thing, he's just totally into it and extremely good. He plays things that people have forgotten exist! Kate would say, "we need such and such a sound" and Paddy would rifle through his things and come up with some old instrument that no one had ever heard of. It made the sound she wanted, though. She was very lucky to have him.'

Andrew Powell adds, 'If you suddenly came up with an idea and said "Look, there's this instrument called a 'whatever'," and she hadn't heard of it, she'd become fascinated to see what it would do. That probably comes partly from her family's background – her brother Paddy is quite interested in collecting various strange plucked string instruments (he actually builds some of them himself), so she's had this background in the family of an interest in slightly unusual and unconventional instruments.'

40

'In Search Of Peter Pan' is one of the best songs on the album, (it is not difficult to imagine Kate Bush as a bit of a 'Peter Pan' herself,) and she develops here a theme that appeared in some of her earlier work – keeping alive the child that is in everyone. 'Kashka From Baghdad' is the celebration of a homosexual with a secret lover, with a whimsical chorus; '*At night they're seen/Laughing loving/They know the way/To be happy*'. Oddly enough, when asked to perform one of the tracks from *Lionheart* on the UK children's show 'Ask Aspel', she chose this number rather than 'In The Warm Room', as she thought the subject matter of the latter was too explicit. How she thought a song about two gay lovers frolicking in the moonlight was more suitable is a good question.

'Wow' is perhaps the most successful song on the album, full of the superlatives that characterize Kate's spoken word: Wow, incredible, unbelievable, fantastic, cool, amazing. The irony is that the song *is* incredible. She says '*I am playing the part of a movie star*'. This movie star sleeps her way to the top, accompanied by a failed homosexual actor who is '*too busy hitting the vaseline*'. She denies any prejudice against homosexuals, explaining: 'There are an awful lot of homosexuals in the business. But that is just an observation, not a criticism.' It is obvious that Kate is much more aware of her surroundings and has a better sense of 'streetsmart' than is evident in her earlier songs. The musical arrangement for 'Wow' is as powerful as that in her first singles, and she is again successful with her use of a strong, memorable chorus, simple, but cleverly devised.

'Hammer Horror' was another track that was pulled for release as a single. Kate Bush explains the story behind it: 'It was quite a complicated story. An actor had a part in a movie but he died on the set, and the current actor was being haunted by the actor before. I was quite enchanted by the whole thing of movies and movie sets and ham actors, and they are very superstitious places as well, theatres and movie people.' The song is a melodramatic exaggerated number in which Kate again uses her voice to its theatrical best. The soft verses are juxtaposed with a vibrant and rousing chorus incorporating an excellent use of percussion and bass. Again, Kate's wild imagination had taken over. The 'Hammer Horror' video was a theatrical event and her performance of this number in her live shows can only be described as spectacular.

41

She does not let anyone down on the rock and roll score either. 'Don't Push Your Foot On The Heartbrake' is a lively, upbeat, if somewhat soul-searching song, and she screeches, with great success, to '*Oh, come on, come on, you've got to use your flow*'. Other tracks on the album include 'Coffee Homeground' and 'Fullhouse', both very different but excellent works. 'Coffee Homeground' has a distinctly 'circus' beat and she playfully accuses her counterpart of poisoning her and the plumber who 'went missing last week'. It's a lot of fun. Her vocals are generally exaggerated, and she adopts farcical ethnic accent.

While Kate was in Nice recording the album, 'The Man With The Child In His Eyes' hit its chart peak at number 6 in the UK, while *The Kick Inside* was re-released with its new sleeve in the USA. For the first time, 'Wuthering Heights' was released as a single over there and some media attention was finally received. Back in the studio in London preparing the final remixes, Kate was astonished to find herself a high-profile personality. Jon Kelly says: 'Suddenly she was famous . . . although it didn't seem to make much difference to her as a person.' Her life, however, had changed. He goes on: 'When we were making *The Kick Inside*, nobody knew who she was so it was quite easy to wander up and down Oxford Street or anywhere else at will and no-one would recognize her. When we were doing the second record it was much harder. She would still offer, if we were hungry, to go out and get the sandwiches. We just couldn't let her, we'd have to send somebody out with her.' He adds; 'There were always people waiting outside Abbey Road for her when she came in. She had a very strong devotée of fans. I think the fact that she lost her privacy and couldn't go out to restaurants or out in the evening without being recognized, or just walk down the street, was more or less what affected her the most.'

Despite her reputation as being something of an introvert as far as her private life was concerned, Kate appeared to like the initial trappings of success, and was genuinely interested to meet her fans and to sign autographs. Jon Kelly says: 'If you were wandering through an airport or something with her, people would just keep stopping her. She actually seemed quite pleased and would not just sign an autograph and throw a bit of paper back at them, but she would actually talk to people insofar as it is possible. It gets very

42

difficult if you've got sixty people waiting to talk to you and there's a plane due to leave in three minutes.'

Only days after completing the final mix of *Lionheart*, Kate was rushed off to Australia to co-host with then-superstar Lief Garrett on the 10th annual 'TV Week' 'King of Pop' Awards where she appeared before two million viewers and performed 'Hammer Horror' live. Jon Kelly was impressed by her ability to keep going: 'Inevitably she was fairly exhausted by the time she'd finished the record because she had been rushing around all over the place. I mean, she left during the last mix to fly to Australia and she never heard the final result until it was released.' On 27 October, EMI released 'Hammer Horror' as Kate's third single in the UK, and a week later it entered the charts at an astonishingly low 73.

Before taking off again on a promotional tour of the Netherlands and Germany, Kate took on the expert assistance of Antony van Laast of the London Contemporary Dance Company. He worked with her for the 'Hammer Horror' video and towards her tour, the date of which was approaching.

Van Laast remembers his work with Kate: 'I worked with Keef MacMillan and had done videos for him prior to the States and I was sitting in a Turkish bath – Porchester Baths – and I phoned my wife at home and she said "There's a message from Keef MacMillan – would you please, as quickly as possible, go over to a rehearsal; he's doing a video with Kate Bush; he needs a man and would you go over and be the man with Kate Bush". So that night I went over to the Festival Ballet Studios and we put together "Hammer Horror". I mean "Hammer Horror" as a dance existed in some kind of form because I believe she had done it in Australia before, but I think we modified it for us, and that's really how we met. We did "Hammer Horror" for the video and then very shortly after that we went to San Remo and we danced it there and then we went over to Munich and we danced it for German television. That's how I first met Kate Bush.

'I'd always been pretty knocked out by the woman because I'd seen the video of "Wuthering Heights" and I just thought she was very interesting. It was funny actually because the person I was with at the time turned round to me and said, "You know, she's just the kind of person who would be good for you to work with", and it was a great coincidence that we were brought together. It was one of those things and I think at the time we both helped each other very much.

'I think the choreographic process of "Hammer Horror" was as one could say, the choreographic process of most of the work I did with Kate and that was that she had a very strong idea of what she wanted – she knew exactly what she wanted – and she used me as a sounding board to throw in a few technical tips, and I added my little bit as well. So I think, in the fairest sense of the word, the creative process on "Hammer Horror" was a true collaboration because Kate is very interested in putting together movement ideas, but perhaps sometimes she needs to work with someone who is a little bit more experienced to help her bring her ideas to fruition.

'Having done this, we were flying back . . . at the time I was only a little dancer with the London Contemporary Dance Theatre, and then I was met by this huge stretched limo and whisked off to the airport at Heathrow, and we got on a little private plane and went to Munich. It was absolutely luxurious and I was being paid for it as well. On the way back from Munich, Kate said to me that she was thinking of doing a tour and would I be interested in helping her at that time with giving her a dance class every day, and helping her with her ideas for the tour, and also would I find her the dancers . . . find the boys whom I thought would be suitable to work with her on the tour. And that's how we started. We started off rehearsing directly after . . . around the time of "Hammer Horror".'

Lionheart was launched in November at the 14th-century castle Ammersoyen in Holland for over two hundred members of the Press and EMI Europe. The invitation explained this great expense by noting that it was 'in keeping with the prestige of the artist'. Their near-child wonder was making them a lot of money. After the reception she was presented by the President of the Association of Dutch Phonographical Industries with the prestigious Edison award for the best single of 1978. Still gracious in the starry light of her success, Kate, in her lilting best-suburban-London accent, thanked her parents for 'making her' and EMI for 'promoting' her – in all sincerity!

On 8th November, Kate was presented with two awards at the *Melody Maker* 1978 Poll Awards at the Venue in London. After only one year on the pop scene and barely two albums, Kate was awarded the 'Brightest New Hope' and 'Best Female Single' for 1978. Her success was unprecedented by anyone's standards. And with less than a week off, Kate was back on the promotional trail, touring the record stores across Britain in a series of personal appearances.

Her next stop was on the 'Leo Sayer Show', where she performed 'Don't Push Your Foot On The Heartbrake'. Another tribute to Kate was actress/singer Julie Covington's cover version of 'The Kick Inside', which she dedicated to Kate 'for inspiration'. The media attention was astounding; in fact, she was on the border of being overexposed, as Tony Myatt noted. 'She was being interviewed by everybody. You'd turn the radio on and you'd hear Kate; you'd turn the telly on and you'd either see her or somebody doing an impression of her. It got to saturation point where she was doing everything. But she didn't actually take a break because of that.'

Kate became the darling of the mimics and, surprisingly enough, she was delighted. She told *Company* magazine: 'Faith Brown is hilarious. I couldn't believe it when I saw her do "Wuthering Heights" and "Wow". She'd learned every step of my dance routines. Of course, it's very flattering to be mimicked. The only time it gets bitchy is when they make fun of people's physical imperfections . . . I don't find that amusing at all.' Appparently Kate was so enamoured with Faith Brown's accuracy that she wrote her a four-page letter thanking her!

As 'Hammer Horror' reached its chart peak at an uninspiring number 44, *Lionheart* entered the charts at number 36, an admirable placing for a second album with an unsuccessful first single.

Determined to shatter the indifference of the USA, Kate left in December to promote the release of 'The Man With The Child In His Eyes', moving on to Canada where she was greeted rather more effusively. In the USA she prepared two songs for NBC's 'Saturday Night Live', definitely a step in the right direction, for the show was staple American entertainment and a number of important music success stories had their beginnings there. Mick Jagger and Paul Simon dropped in to see her performance, which only helped to enhance her image as a *cause célèbre*. To her credit, 'The Man With The Child In His Eyes' went ahead and entered the US Billboard Hot Hundred in February of the next year. Although it remained there for four weeks, it only reached number 85. Again she had failed to break completely into the US market.

In January 1979, Kate was voted the Best New Artist of 1978 in the *Record Mirror* National Poll, and in their 'Christmas Music Press Summed Up', Simon Frith of the *Melody Maker* said of Kate: 'Kate Bush's success was a triumph of the romantic will. Her talents are remote, fragmentary, dreams to sustain her housebound listeners through dark winters to come.' The reference was slightly derisory, but Kate's record sales for 1978 were astounding. She was the seventh-bestselling LP artist, while *The Kick Inside* was the tenth-bestselling album of the year. 'Wuthering Heights' clocked in as the eleventh-bestselling single of the year. Her first year at the helm of the public gaze had come to an end: her accomplishment was phenomenal.

The new year opened with dozens of television appearances and an enormous co-production in Switzerland where she appeared on an ABBA special, and for Christmas she filmed a version of 'Wuthering Heights' which had her shrieking à la Julie Andrews, barefoot in the Alps – in the snow! She went on to take part in a BBC phone-in programme on Radio One, 'Personal Call', where she stunned radio operators by jamming incoming lines for over an hour. She was in demand everywhere.

Next on the agenda was the video for 'Wow' directed by Keef MacMillan, who was also responsible for her 'Wuthering Heights', 'The Man With The Child In His Eyes' and 'Hammer Horror' videos. In the video she appears in a purple lycra dress and her sensuality is undeniable as she minces and prances across the set. Increasing her reputation as sex symbol of pop, she is blatantly sexual in her interpretation of the star who sleeps her way to the top, which consequently leads to her being labelled 'raunchy' and 'wanton'.

During all of this Kate was making the preparations for the live tour: the performances were set to begin on 2nd April. On 4th March, Kate was honoured with the award for Best British Newcomer and Best British Female Vocalist at the Capital Radio Annual Awards. Just days later her tour was declared sold out, and for the first time the public would see the real thing – Kate Bush Live. With a year of acolades and awards behind her, the greatest test still remained – could she captivate an audience?

46

5
THE TOUR

You flow around all that comes in your way
Don't think it over it always takes you over
And sets your spirit dancing

'Moving'
Kate Bush, 1978

After more than twelve months in the public eye, the live tour was to mark the first time that Kate Bush had actually performed in front of a live audience. The build-up in the media was stupendous. Critics from the Press and radio speculated that Ms Bush had never yet performed live because she relied on the special effects that only mixing in a studio can produce. The quality of her film work and videos only added to the pressure on Kate, and fans waiting with bated breath to discover if she would cast the same spell on stage as she did on disc. Kate said, 'People expect a certain standard from me. I have been built up over the last year and now I want to give them everything I have got'.

Planning for the tour had actually begun in January 1979 when Kate first conceived the concept for the show. She intended it to be an extravaganza that would weave together poetry, song, music and dance in an entirely new way. Because of her output of highly stylistic promotional videos and vignettes, Kate had so far managed to escape the need for touring. On 2nd January, David Jackson, the production designer, along with Kate, Paddy and Del Palmer, met at her family home, Wickham Farm, for artistic and script discussions, the first of meetings that would recur for over a month. Dates for the tour were set for the beginning of April and the recruitment of crew and band members got underway.

47

Hilary Walker, Kate's agent, took on Richard Aimes as tour manager at an early stage. Aimes had managed tours for artists like Duran Duran, Paul McCartney, Steve Harley and Peter Gabriel, a star-studded line-up into which Kate was neatly fitted. He remembers the initial stages of the tour: 'I was brought in by Hilary Walker who looks after Kate's affairs along with Kate's family; this was at a fairly early stage. Kate had never done a live show before, although she'd done a few TVs and videos and by this time had three hit records. Kate and the Bushes wanted something a bit special and anyone who saw the video that was released after the show would realize it was a bit different from a band just going out on the road and playing live. It was more theatrical with the show being broken up, in the end, into three acts, and from the beginning there was a very long process of rehearsals, not only for Kate and the musicians but also the choreography for the dancers, all the scenery and even a magician.'

The cast for the show included the KT Bush Band of whom the original members – Paddy Bush, Del Palmer and Brian Bath – played mandolin, bass guitar and rhythm guitar respectively. Added to this highly successful trio was Kevin McNally on keyboards and the saxophone, Preston Hayman on drums, Alan Murphy on guitar and Ben Barson for additional keyboards. Dancers Gary Hurst and Stewart Arnold were hired by choreographer Anthony van Laast, with whom she had worked on the 'Hammer Horror' video. Simon Drake, the famous illusionist, provided magic and illusions. Drake was credited with working for Howard Jones, Steve Miller, Julian Lennon and had also appeared twice with the Royal Ballet at the Royal Opera House. It was a talented team, made up of the very best in theatre and popular music and not surprisingly Kate found herself with a case of the jitters at the thought of working with these gurus of the entertainment world.

Production began immediately, with rehearsals for all members of the crew. Preston Hayman, the drummer, recalls: 'It was certainly a tour which took a lot of planning and a long time to execute. We rehearsed for about six months – usually with a tour you'd rehearse for about three or four weeks – and this was the first time to my knowledge that someone had fused a mixture of dance, music, magic and mime on tour. It turned out to be a very special time for me, very

48

memorable. Our first meeting was at the Farm, at the small studio they had there, and it was very laid-back. There was just Kate, Brian, Paddy and Del and they made me feel very much at ease. We went through a few numbers and recorded them, and it was a very pleasant afternoon with lots of cups of tea and Mrs Bush coming up with the biscuits. The family really like tea and cake and biscuits and things – it's all very civilized.' Rehearsals began at Woodwharf studios in Greenwich.

Alan Murphy of John Baldry fame was the guitarist, and it was the first time that he had worked with Kate. It was a relationship that was developed extensively as he continued to work on the remainder of Kate Bush's albums. When he turned up for his audition, he didn't even know who Kate was. He says, 'I had missed the whole "Wuthering Heights" thing as I'd been in America and Canada with John Baldry and I didn't really know who she was. I went along to the farm and we had a play. There was quite a queue of guitar players. I remember that I had a good time. There were buckets of tea coming in (as there always is at Kate's) and Kit Kats and things. It was a couple of weeks later I got the call and it was positive – we were doing the tour. That was the beginning of quite a long rehearsal stint which was all done in Greenwich – about five or six months at rehearsals for the one and only tour we've done.'

As in the past, the entire Bush family took an avid interest in the production of the tour, and supported Kate and the entire crew from beginning to end. Alan explains: 'It was a kind of family feeling – so many of us. Everybody was very green at the beginning and gradually absorbed all the influences that Kate dishes out. She gradually pulled us all together into quite a tight-knit community.'

Because of this unique and very personal atmosphere, the crew got along famously and much of the success of that original tour has been attributed to the fact that everyone liked Kate enormously. She took it upon herself, as did the rest of her family, to make every member of the group feel involved, and spent time explaining to everyone exactly how she saw the tour and what each of their parts would be in the creation. Tour manager Richard Aimes adds to the picture of the highly creative and warm atmosphere: 'While the dancers and the band were rehearsing, we were putting the show together, over-seeing the financial side of things with the Bushes and all the normal preparations for going on the road, including booking hotels, sorting out the lighting and the sound, along with special effects. From my side of things, the incredible thing about the tour was the fact that there were about forty of us altogether, twenty in the band party and about twenty in the crew, and I'd never experienced such a family atmosphere on the road before. It was just everyone giving their all to help make the show the success that it was. Kate had this incredible knack of giving it her all and giving herself to the project in hand and people just latch on to that and want to help her. It was just a natural instinct. People wanted to get it right every time. It was an incredible experience seeing forty people being so into the whole project and so behind Kate.'

Three months before the tour was scheduled to begin, rehearsals started in earnest and Kate began rehearsing six days a week for up to fourteen hours a day. Hilary Walker noted, 'She was involved at every stage, organizing costumes, lighting, choreography and music.' Antony Van Laast remembers the strenuous months before the tour and the part Kate had to play in her own choreography: 'It was a very long rehearsal period, and strange really because being a dancer one is used to working from 10am until 6pm but Kate used to start at about 4pm and work until 2 in the morning. It was a very exciting process. Kate would arrive with very strong ideas on what she wanted and I had these two fantastic boys, Gary Hurst and Stewart Arnold, and we would put the whole show together. I can't emphasize the word "collaboration" enough because when you're working with a trained dancer, the choreographer is usually very much the master, but part of Kate's fascination is her idiosyncratic way of moving and you can't take that away. When I put the two boys in they would do a very "Kate Bush-type" performance. We took whatever Kate felt was the right move and developed it and orchestrated it.'

The dress rehearsals began at the Rainbow Theatre in London two weeks before the actual performance. The secrecy surrounding the tour was phenomenal. Not one member of the Press was given the slightest inkling of what her stage act would constitute. Agendas passed among members of the crew had printed on them a cartoon of a pirate saying, 'Have the walls got ears here?' and a sub note, 'You don't need me to tell you that most information contained in this

50

bulletin is confidential, do you?' One overly avid photographer managed to slip into the studio where Kate was rehearsing, but before any worthwhile shots were taken his film was confiscated and he was severely reprimanded. The tour was to be a complete surprise. Kate remarked that it was like giving a 'present' to her fans, all wrapped up and not to be opened until she presented it herself.

Aside from the normal last-minute technical problems, the final preparations were nearly complete. A microphone was specially designed to be attached to Kate's head so that she could move freely across the stage keeping her arms free for the dance and mime numbers while singing at the same time. She noted, 'When I've got the head set and I'm moving a lot it's an amazing feeling of freedom, because there's nothing in your hands, yet you can hear your voice being projected miles away. Its incredible.'

Kate's whole family continued to assist the unit before they hit the road. Kate's sister-in-law, John Bush's wife, helped with the cooking, most of which was vegetarian. The rest of the family took care of the managerial aspects and were constantly around for moral and creative support. Simon Drake says, 'Looking back I remember that my first impression of Kate and her family was that the whole family were a very musical bunch and very much behind Kate. It did take some time to dawn on me but it was very much the Bush family involvement as opposed to just Kate Bush. Paddy was very much on the musical side and is someone who plays a lot of antique instruments – mandolin and hurdy-gurdy. He was fascinated, possibly obsessed, with these wonderful old boxes with bits of string coming out of them. Jay – well he is more on the business side and perhaps lyrically as well, and he is also a photographer. And of course, Ma and Pa were often there supporting them.'

A near-disaster with the ramp at the beginning of 'Strange Phenomena' was the only incident that marred an otherwise perfect run of rehearsals. Simon Drake explained: 'Kate and two of the dancers would come in under the ramp as I was going out from underneath it. The whole thing was surrounded by these flashing lights – you needed about three roadies to counterbalance it. Anyway, it slipped and landed on my head. The only lucky part was that I missed part of the aluminium framework by about a foot and I remember going half under and waking up on the floor with Kate over me going "Are you OK?" which was quite nice.'

The practices were complete. The sets and screens and special effects equipment were loaded up with the whole crew and taken down to Poole in Dorset where there was to be a two-hour set in front a live audience the night before the official opening in Liverpool on 2nd April. It was an amazing show, with different films and slides on three screens, Antony Van Laast, the dancers, Simon Drake and the 7-piece band backing Kate herself. The show was a wild success. Everything worked perfectly. The months of orchestration were so effective that not one cue was missed. It was a glorious beginning to Kate Bush's first tour. Until tragedy struck, the kind of tragedy that could have ruined the entire tour.

Bill Duffield was a highly acclaimed and popular lighting designer who had worked previously with Steve Harley and Peter Gabriel. Because of a few last-minute problems with cues, Richard Aimes called him in to help out. He was very successful and very well-established, and was able to put a bit of magic into the light show. Richard Aimes remembers the tragedy: 'We returned to the hotel after a very successful show and everyone was having a few drinks and was pretty "up", and then I got a call from the hall to say that Bill had run back up to where the desk was placed at the top of the auditorium and was doing what's called the "idiot check" – you just go back onto the stage after everything is in the truck and make sure that nothing is forgotten. Somebody from the auditorium had lifted up a panel from the flooring on the very last step of the central aisle and left the cover on the step before it. Bill rushed up and as it wasn't lit very well, tripped over it and fell head first down seventeen feet onto concrete. The ensuing week was terrible because he was rushed to hospital and put on a life-support machine for about a week. I went down personally to try to help the police and the hospital in locating his parents. He lasted only a week.'

The whole crew was shattered. What had been a spectacular preview of Kate's debut tour was now cast in darkness and it was difficult for anyone to go on. Simon Drake continues: 'Kate was shattered, and in fact it felt as if the whole tour was going to collapse. Everything so far had gone so well with the stageing, the dancing,

Kate at sixteen – just beginning (above). (*Camera Press, London*)

Behind the scenes of the German 'Bio's Banhof' in 1978 (right). (*Rex Features, London*)

The Tour of Life 1979.
Kate appears alone
and with the 'Mad
Violinist' – Simon
Drake. The KT Bush
Band back. (Alone,
Camera Press, London)

Capital Radio Awards 1980 with Alan Freeman. Kate won Best Female Vocalist for 1979 (left). (*The Photo Source, London*)

Capital Radio Awards 1980 with Kenny Everett (below). (*The Photo Source, London*)

On stage backed by the KT Bush Band; boyfriend Del Palmer on the right (opposite above). (*Rex Features, London*)

August 1985, on German television, Kate performs *Running Up That Hill* (opposite below). (*David Redfern, London*)

Army Dreamers, 1980. The famous 'mop maid' from her German promotion (above) and the highly acclaimed video shot (below). (*London Features International*)

Hammer Horror, (above) and *Babooshka* (right), 1980. (*Camera Press and London Features International*)

Promoting the
Single File box and
video, December
1983 (above).
(*London Features
International*)

Kate Bush and
boyfriend Del
Palmer, 1984 (left).
(*Rex Features,
London*)

Kate Bush with
comedians Lenny
Henry and Jennifer
Saunders in the
promotion following
the release of the *Comic
Relief Christmas Book*,
October 1986 (above).
(*International Features,
London*)

Kate Bush with Peter
Gabriel at the BPI
awards 1987. Bush
captured Best Female
Vocalist for 1986 (left).
(*International Features,
London*)

the theatrics, the music, the illusions, and now, twenty-four hours before the opening night, a tragedy such as this had struck.'

Richard Aimes adds: 'At that point, the whole feeling of the tour could have collapsed. I think everyone thought Bill was a professional like the rest of us, and I think any professional would have wanted the thing to carry on, expecially for Kate as it was her first ever live performance. I don't think anyone will ever forget it. At the same time, however, it brought everyone together ever so closely right from the beginning.' Despite the obvious tears and misgivings that followed the terrible accident, the crew pulled themselves together, collected the equipment and headed for Liverpool. 'We did it for Bill,' said Aimes later.

The show was a stunning success. No-one had ever expected the squeaky-voiced, sparrow-like Kate Bush to control and manipulate an audience the way she did. The reviewers were spellbound. The *Liverpool Post* said: 'Kate Bush is a love affair, a poignant exposition of the bridges of dreams that link the adulated and the adoring'. Moving on to Birmingham, the *Evening Echo* glowed: 'Kate Bush's eerie dance and mime works twice as well on stage as on "Top of the Pops". Mike Davies of *Melody Maker* wrote: 'The most magnificent spectacle I've ever encountered in the world of rock . . . Kate Bush is the sort of performer for whom the word "superstar" is belittling'. The *Oxford Times* confirmed: 'Yeah, Kate Bush . . . you're amazing'.

Kate Bush continued to splendid reviews as she travelled to Southampton, Bristol, Manchester, Sunderland and Edinburgh. For her final performances on the UK tour, she played five nights at the London Palladium before going on to the continent. During her tour, 'Wow' had climbed to number 14 in the singles charts where it was to remain for over three weeks. Kate Bush was a smash success.

Before the tour began, Kate had expressed nervousness at the thought of playing the London Palladium for her first tour. 'I am terrified, not because of the audience, but because I might not be good enough,' she had said, 'but if you're going to start somewhere that seems as good a place as any'.

The London Press displayed no such reservations: 'A dazzling testimony to a remarkable talent', shouted John Coldstream of the *Daily Telegraph*. 'Kate Bush lines up all the old stereotypes, mows them down and hammers them into a coffin with a show that is, quite literally, stunning,' wrote Thorsen Prentice of the *Daily Mail*, and the *Record Mirror* claimed it was 'the best welding of rock and theatrical presentation that we are ever likely to see.' She had passed the test with flying colours. As the response was so great she added three dates to the end of her European tour for appearances at the Hammersmith Odeon. One of the dates, 12th May 1979, was to be a benefit for Bill Duffield. Peter Gabriel and Steve Harley would appear for the performance, both having been friends and colleagues of the late lighting designer.

But first the European tour began. Simon Drake describes the show: 'One of the sections was Kate playing songs on piano and the others included the dancers and dance routines with Kate singing. Then there was me with the illusions and tricks going on while Kate sang, and in some numbers she performed, like "L'Amour", there were these floating balls going around on the stage and these illusions that I had to perform. There was "In Search Of Peter Pan" where I played a sort of Puck character – Puck rock we called it at the time. I had pointed ears and a wig and floated this silver ball all over the place – which raised a few laughs – and there was "Strange Phenomena" where there was the stick floating around the stage. Another part was where I had to walk through a mirror. When Kate performed the number "Violin" I donned a wig and frantically started playing a violin faster and faster and eventually smoke would start coming out of it all over the stage. In fact, the violin was Paddy's old school violin. In fact, it was during that number you could see Paddy dressed as a cello.' It amused Simon that the critics of the Bush tour imagined that he was seven or eight different people because of his vast variety of guises. Simon Drake was, of course, the 'Mad Violinist' who captivated the critics with his wild, exhaustive leaping and spinning on the stage.

The Europeans lapped the show up. Kate contracted a minor throat ailment which caused the Stockholm concerts, the first on the tour, to be cut short by several numbers: she wasn't allowed to talk to anyone because of the strain on her voice and it was necessary to miss out most of the second act. But the audience loved it. The other singers, many with opera training, covered for Kate in her weak spots. Richard Aimes notes: 'One interesting thing about that tour was Kate's backing singers – the female backing singers. We had to get people who could perform opera in order to hit the incredibly high notes and they'd never been on a tour like this in their lives.'

From Stockholm, Kate travelled over the next three weeks to Copenhagen, Hamburg, Amsterdam, Stuttgart, Munich, Cologne, Paris, Mannheim and Frankfurt before returning to London. Her concerts were a sell-out in every city and the excitement never dimmed. Kate was toted as the best female pop star of Europe, and the best thing ever to come from the UK. While Kate was in Amsterdam for two performances, she was awarded the Dutch Ivor Novello award for 'Wuthering Heights', being nominated three times in the best song musically and lyrically categories for 'Wuthering Heights' and 'The Man With The Child In His Eyes'. Shortly afterwards, Peter Gabriel and Steve Harley flew over at their own expense to rehearse for the benefit performance. It was the first time that Peter Gabriel and Kate Bush had met aside from a brief encounter when Gabriel attended her Palladium performance with his wife Jill. Simon Drake remembers Kate asking him about Gabriel because she knew he had been a Genesis fan for years. A relationship developed that is still strong, both personally and professionally.

The benefit concert in London on 12th May was an extremely emotional event. Steve Harley of Cockney Rebel and solo fame recalls the evening: 'In itself it was incredibly moving because Kate and Peter sang one of my songs, and Peter and I sang one of Kate's together, which was "The Man With The Child In His Eyes". – we called it "The Woman With The Child In Her Eyes" – and Kate and I sang one of Peter's, so it was pretty exciting to be there doing background vocals on my own song while some hugely talented person sang it. After the show, Billy's parents, and I think a brother or sister, came backstage. In meeting them I shall never forget the passionate gratitude – the *depth* of passion in their gratitude is the best way I can phrase it. The look in their eyes . . . the thanks . . . it was the best thing I've ever done in my life.'

The second evening of the performance was videotaped and released as 'Kate Bush Live At Hammersmith Odeon' along with a four-track EP, *Kate Bush Live On Stage*. Using an outside mobile recording truck, the performance was recorded and retained as it happened.

Richard Aimes remembers how Kate would always put her heart and soul into everything she did. She would act a song, acting as any great performer does. Kate herself said, 'Music *is* expression for me. When I perform I am definitely someone else – someone a lot stronger. When I am on stage I get, I don't know, possessed, really away from it.'

Antony Van Laast feels that Kate's tour was one of the landmarks in British pop. He notes, 'I think Bowie will always be looked upon as a landmark in pop theatre, and I think Kate was the next mark after that. Still now people talk about the Kate Bush show at the London Palladium. It broke a lot of barriers and it's all to Kate's credit, totally. I think she's very clever.'

So pleased and content were the crew that they went to great expense to round up the final show with a series of traditional practical jokes. During 'Wow', as Kate and two men in long skirts danced about in a dry ice fog, one of the crew members appeared dressed in a frogman's outfit at the end of the quay, and began dancing with the two dancers. Aimes laughs: 'How Kate didn't stop! ... it was an incredible piece of professionalism for her because it was so funny.' Another funny event took place during 'Egypt' when two of the crew trollopped across the stage in a rented camel suit. Richard Aimes adds: 'They were only going to be on the stage for about half a minute, just for a laugh, but Kate wouldn't let them off. She got hold of the camel's neck and pulled the camel round the stage while she sang the whole of the song. For the most part the jokes were very subtle ones. If the audience did see them, they would appreciate them. It wasn't going to be a disturbance for them as far as the show was concerned. Another thing that happened was that a guy dressed up in a top hat and tails on a sit-up-and-beg bicycle and just cycled straight across the stage in the middle of a number. There were some great laughs, and in fact I've never seen a crew go to that extent before. They really had thought this out and put it into the context of the performance which I think goes to show how everybody loved her an awful lot and just wanted to join in the last laugh. It was amazing how everybody on that tour was working for one thing, to make the show a success.'

Simon Drake also commented on the hard work and the admirable manner in which the crew handled it: 'When we were on that tour I felt terribly sorry for the roadies who had to truck all the props around the countryside, including the giant ramp that I mentioned earlier. There was also a giant egg which was lined with red velvet – an enormous heavy thing, and it rolled onto the stage with Kate Bush ensconced in it going upside down, which was quite amazing. They must have had a great time trying to take that around. And there was this big barrel with "Pork" written on it which was used for a part which I played, Hugo the Mad Poisoner. It was all part of the routine where I was trying to strangle Kate and poison her in "Hammer Horror". But they never complained; no-one quit; in fact, they were always smiling.' Richard Aimes confirms: 'Some of them actually came up to me after the performances and said "I'll do the next one for free if I can do it".'

It was over. Fraught with exhaustion, both mental and physical, Kate Bush took the following two weeks off to relax. During this time *The Kick Inside* went platinum. Having won the hearts of Europe and the UK, Kate Bush Live had proved to be worth waiting for. Her success was exemplary. Whether it was just a question of EMI's good planning, or Kate's unmitigated energetic efforts, her career had taken off in two years, making her the most popular female singer, some say of all time, in the UK.

6
ENCORE

Time and time again
Line and line again
Ooh yeah you're amazing
                    'Wow'
        Kate Bush, 1978

In June 1979, Kate began work on her third album, making clear to EMI that this time she would be working at her own speed. She was feeling shell-shocked after the frenzy of the tour and the publicity that inevitably followed, so after mixing the live tapes from her Hammersmith appearance, with the help of Jon Kelly, she slipped out of the limelight, aside from very few appearances, for several months.

The Hammersmith performance was mixed to produce a four-track EP, released as *Kate Bush Live On Stage*, with 'Them Heavy People' as the lead track. Because of the fruitful partnership she had developed with Jon Kelly, it was natural for him to continue his work as co-producer and engineer on the third album. She moved immediately to Air Studios to begin work. Alan Murphy, her lead guitarist, remembers: 'I felt like we hadn't stopped touring – it just felt that we'd moved the tour up to Air Studios, basically, and we'd only augmented with one or two other people, Max Middleton for instance, who played a lot of piano on the tracks. It was just the next step from the tour and it went on for about six months.'

Max Middleton was primarily a session musician, famous for his work with the Rolling Stones. He was brought in to take over some of the instrumentation from Kate, and to add a new and different flavour to the keyboards. He was surprised at Kate's talent. 'Not having met her, and only ever having heard "Wuthering Heights", I had a preconceived idea of what she might be like – you know, a girl with a strange voice and maybe an obscure single that was just one lucky one. But when I met her I completely reversed my opinion. She's a fantastic person, and fantastic in the way she writes her music also – her music is a lot deeper than it is on the surface . . . you really have to go into her music. There are a lot of subjects she draws inspiration from. I just thought she was some silly girl singing but there's a lot more to her than that.'

The album, *Never For Ever*, makes use of various instruments from Paddy Bush's seemingly endless medieval collection and introduces the Fairlight CMI (Computerized Musical Instrument) synthesizer, typically remembered for its use by Peter Gabriel. Stephen Paine, Gabriel's cousin and a synthesizer session player, describes the technology behind the Fairlight and the sounds it enables a musician to create: 'What the Fairlight was doing was incredibly basic. It was able to record a sound and play it back on the keyboard at any pitch, polyphonically and as chords. Up to then something similar only existed on the Mellotron.' Gabriel was in fact the first person to use the Fairlight in a British recording studio and subsequently set up a company, Synco Systems, which had exclusive rights to import it.

Kate was introduced to the magic of the Fairlight in January 1980 when she worked with Gabriel on his third solo album. He called upon her talents to back for 'Games Without Frontiers' and 'No Self Control', and contributed to Kate's expansion in the use of traditional instrumentation. As a result *Never For Ever* has a characteristically Gabriel sound. Gabriel influenced Kate through-out her ensuing albums, specifically on *The Dreaming*, on which she used the Gabriel/Collins-created sound which prohibits all use of cymbals.

Falling short again on new songs for the album, Kate was forced to dig up some of the earlier songs she had created. Alan Murphy found the difference between her old and new material quite marked. 'I remember at one stage we were a couple of songs short and it meant Kate digging a little deeper into her past to resurrect a few things, and one of the ones she pulled out was "Violin". That sticks quite strongly in my mind because it was quite a young-sounding song, quite rocky, and I always remember the way we had to record that.

It was quite unlike the other things we did which were much more grown up.'

'Violin' is reminiscent of 'The Saxophone Song' on her first album. Kate uses her voice to its screeching extreme as she emulates the sound of a violin. With a speedier tempo than most of her earlier songs, 'Violin' is more of a traditional rock number, far less controlled than the remaining tracks on the album. Her attempt to use her voice as a violin results in a squeaking, twanging track sounding more like a sadistic exploitation of vocal chords than a song. The lyrics rely heavily on interspersed references to Nero, Paganini and BVs (in all likelihood *Beata Virgo*, the blessed Virgin). It is a coy, devilish attempt to breathe a little fire into a staid violin, but in many ways it fails because of the song's lack of melody.

While she was recording, Kate was asked to participate in a concert to celebrate the seventy-fifth anniversary of the London Symphony Orchestra. Cliff Richard was billed with her to perform in front of a full house at the Royal Albert Hall in London. She was initially reluctant to take part. 'It's a terrific honour, but I thought about turning it down. I mean, it's a bit high-brow . . . But then I thought I'd look stuck up if I did.' She did the performance, singing three songs, including the first performance of 'Blow Away', the song she wrote for Bill Duffield. 'Blow Away' also appears on *Never For Ever* and has a thoughtful, touching melody that takes a look at where musicians go when they die. In distinct contrast to 'Violin', the song is lady-like and refined, with a soft vocal and the increasingly evident use of the Fairlight. The performance at the Albert Hall was a success, with Simon Kinnersly of the *Daily Mail* noting, 'Miss Bush was in breathtaking form . . . she emerged as the only star'. And as if to confirm the fact, Kate was awarded the Best Female Singer Award for the second year running at the *Melody Maker* Annual Poll Awards dinner at London's Waldorf Hotel.

To take advantage of the pre-Christmas record-buying rush, Kate recorded 'December Will Be Magic Again' for release as a Christmas single. The song is a whimsical celebration of traditional Christ-mases, replete with references to Bing Crosby, Old Saint Nicholas and 'Silent Night'. EMI refused to release it because it lacked the requisite commercial 'punch'. Disappointed, Kate hastily prepared a video for the track, slipping it into the BBC TV 'Winter Snowtime

Special' in place of the previously recorded 'Wuthering Heights' video in which she appeared barefoot in the snow in the Swiss Alps.

In late November, Kate, along with Peter Townsend and Joe Brown, sang backing vocals for Lesley Duncan's 'Sing Children Sing', a recording from which all profits would go to the United Nations Year of the Child fund. 'Kate', a BBC TV special celebrating the talents of Kate Bush appeared on 28th December. Featuring a large proportion of her old repertoire Kate also performed 'Egypt' and 'Violin' as a preview to her new album. She sang a duet with Peter Gabriel for the second time, strengthening a union that would flourish in the years to come. It is likely that this performance finally convinced Gabriel to take Kate on as backing vocalist for the two tracks on *Gabriel III*. They sang one of Roy Harper's new songs, 'Another Day'. Roy Harper was another of EMI's aspiring musicians, less successful in the long run than Bush, but a close friend with whom she later worked on a number of albums, both his and her own.

In January 1980, Kate moved from Air Studios to the legendary Abbey Road, Studio Two, which Max Middleton remembers as being rich with Beatle memories and memorabilia. The production of the album was controlled by Kate, and Andrew Powell, producer of the first two albums, comments: 'I stopped working with her after the second record but she didn't produce the next record all by herself, if I remember; she co-produced it with Jon Kelly, so she still had someone there whom she could trust, as it were, from the initial set-up, the sort of family that had been established on the first two records, which was probably a very good thing before she went completely on her own.' He also remembers that although she was confident of her abilities and her capability to create exactly what she wanted, he worried slightly about her objectivity. 'It may be a good thing, but it can be dangerous, particularly when you have written the songs yourself, you're singing them yourself, your own music and lyrics. I think it can be quite hard to be objective about your own performance of something that has become that personal to you.'

Alan Murphy does remember, though, that Kelly gave Kate quite a free rein: 'Jon Kelly was always . . . not strong, but a good direction, always a very positive engineer/producer, so he helped a lot in that respect. And Kate obviously would either be playing the piano or suggesting things.' Jon Kelly described his ideas for the album: 'The third album was very creative, with a lot of experimentation, a lot of trying things and making things work without doing it in the traditional fashion. It's difficult to explain. We really wanted to make the third album simple and effective, but making things simple is sometimes the most difficult thing to do. It was time-consuming and difficult in that respect, but I think we achieved something out of it.'

The recording of *Never For Ever* took five months to complete, much longer than any of Kate's previous works. It is both a tribute to and an expansion of her already remarkable voice and sound, and the album is enriched with an exotic sensitivity. Where *Lionheart* was more an analysis of gut-wrenching emotion, *Never For Ever* is a tribute to Kate's imagination, her ability to meld fantasy and reality into a comprehensive whole, touching on very real human feelings and fears without transporting them into the realm of the surreal.

Max Middleton admits that he found it a bit difficult with Kate taking on some of the direction, probably because she had, as she had in the past, a total idea of what the tracks should sound like from the moment of their conception. A piano player herself, releasing some of the work to Middleton was predictably a difficult task. He says, 'I know I found it a little difficult because I was used to playing with musicians who would just shout out a few chord symbols and we'd play. The words were very important to Kate, and when she wrote tunes I think she saw the whole thing. She saw the words, the music and how she would actually perform them on stage. Not many people actually think like that. Most people are glad enough if they can get a tune recorded – they're not thinking about performance. I found it a little bit difficult because we would do a take and she would say that it wasn't quite right but she couldn't tell us what was wrong. You know, if someone says to me, "You're playing a wrong chord", I understand that; or "It should be faster or slower", I understand; but the things she was talking about I couldn't come to grips with.'

Aware that she was trying the patience of her band members and engineers, Kate made sure she remained confident and friendly to everyone, and she is remembered as dealing with all aspects of the production with a fair hand, a 'gentle, guiding hand, never forceful.'

Middleton remembers a time when they had spent far too long on one track and everyone was beginning to get a little irritable: 'I think Jon Kelly was losing his patience a little bit and I noticed that as he was speaking through the microphone to the two musicians in the studio, he was really directing all his speech to Alan [Murphy]. After three or four hours of directing everything to Alan, Kate went up to Jon and whispered, "Occasionally make some suggestion to Brian [Bath] too because he's going more and more in the shadow and he's probably starting to feel a little bit upset." It was just a little thing, but she was obviously concerned with the feelings of everybody and to me those small things were very important. I've seen the opposite in studios when people are terribly rude and of course it has the opposite effect. She was very good, I thought, with people.'

As usual, there was no individual in the crew who had anything other than glowing reports to make about Kate. The recording was slow and painstaking, and as Max Middleton noticed, she was vague in her direction, not knowing precisely what tack to take in the development of the songs. Kelly noted that she was a perfectionist, happy to sing the same things over and over again for a whole day, persevering until she was absolutely happy. Bringing in Max Middleton was one of the first attempts she made to break away from the pattern that had developed over the first two albums, where Kate would play the song at the piano and maybe sing along, and the band would play with her. Kelly felt that to a certain extent that governed the form of the song. The break from this strategem is obvious in tracks like 'The Infant Kiss' where feeling the limitations of the song she began to experiment. Relinquishing some of her adamant directives, Kate allowed Max Middleton to come up with much of the jazzy blocks of 'Egypt'. He remembers feeling relieved that he was given a little room in which to allow his creativity to take over. 'I liked "Egypt" because I was allowed to play a little bit more on that. It's very difficult her being a piano player and I had to play electric piano. She comes in with a song and plays note for note every time she plays that particular song. Basically I come from a jazz and blues background, I like to have a certain amount of improvisation and there's not really a lot of call for that when you're playing with Kate, except in "Egypt". I managed to have a bit of a blow and I wrote a little instrumental passage. I think it was 7/4 time and she couldn't play it at first, but I showed her how to play it and she mastered that after a few days and that was quite good fun.' Kate does acknowledge Middleton's work and his influence on her piano compositions.

If some members of the band found her direction far too vague to comprehend, Alan Murphy was not one of them. 'She would always use some quite interesting picture to describe what she wanted to hear from your part, which some people would find quite difficult to work to, but I always found it really helpful. Some people would find it vague – I found it open enough to let my kind of colour in and of course, if it doesn't work, or she doesn't like it, then she's only got to say "not quite". I think she, more than anyone, has grown to understand that if you limit someone you also limit the form.'

Kate herself describes the difficulties in getting across her image of what the complete track should sound like from all facets: 'I think everything is part of the picture, and with instruments you're really putting in the colour, and trying to create an atmosphere. It's hard to talk about these sort of things because they are to do with sounds being associative and actually creating their own pictures. The lyrics are the whole story really and the rest is, hopefully, what's behind the story. It's hopefully suggesting the subject matter which is creating an atmosphere. It's impossible to analyse it – it comes from so many different sources.'

Her family was again involved in the production of *Never For Ever*. Their presence was helpful and comforting to the members of the crew, and most of them rave about the solidity of Kate's family unit. Although they had, on several occasion, been deemed 'incestuous', Middleton claims that anyone who knew them would realize the strength of the family's relationships and the idiocy of any reference to unnatural practice.

Jon, at this point, was more involved in the accounting side than the day-to-day studio work. He had always been a very strong character in the organization, and was now acting as a record company executive, paying bills and popping in here and there to watch or comment, but really keeping behind the scenes. Of Paddy, Middleton says, 'Paddy was one of these eccentric musicians, I think. He would have a lot of ideas and was into medieval instruments – playing recorders or old mandolins – and I believe

Paddy's wife makes mandolins and lutes and things like that. Pete Townsend has bought stuff from her. Paddy's into all that ethnic stuff and if you go round his house it is like going back to the 60s. He looks a bit wild – I think because he's one of these people who are always talking about things. His mind races quicker than he can talk . . . he's a bit vacant in his eyes, but he's a nice guy as well.' Kate's parents were always supportive of everyone in the band. Alan Murphy remembers Kate's mother in particular. 'Kate's Mum especially has been really warm to me, offering me assistance, you know, when you get down periods. But there's quite a gentle aura about them, they've never intrusive like some of the parents I've seen in quite similar situations to Kate's.'

Middleton recalls fondly an incident that took place at Air Studios, which illustrates quite clearly why Kate Bush is so popular among her colleagues: 'It was just a simple thing, there were about seven or eight of us in the studio and she asked whether we would like a cup of tea. We all said OK, and she said she'd go and make it. Now at Air Studios it's a hell of a trek; most studios have a little kitchen off the studio, but she had to trek quite a long way, go up another floor through other studios into a back room and make the tea. She went away and did that – made a huge pot of tea for us. She could hardly carry the tray and all the cups and biscuits and everything. She struggled in – she's a little tich of a girl – and in the meantime, while she was away, I think a couple of other people came in. She came and put the tray down and everybody selfishly grabbed a cup of tea and left her with nothing. People offered her their tea, but she wouldn't have it, she went up and made another lot.'

The album was completed in March that year. During the final months of production, Kate was drawn back into the public eye, winning a series of awards, astounding both herself and EMI with her incredible success. In January, she was voted Best Female artist of 1979 by *Record Mirror*, Best Female Singer of 1979 in the *New Musical Express* Poll and at the *Music Week* Annual Awards Gala at the Dorchester Hotel in London she was presented with the award for the Top Female Album Artist of 1979. In February, she took time from her own publicity to do some back up vocals for Roy Harper's new album, *Unknown Soldier*, and performed a duet with him, 'You', on *The Game Part III*.

Kate was honoured yet again at the British Rock and Pop Awards ceremony where she won Best Female Singer of 1979. Four days later, she was nominated Best Female Singer of 1979 in the *Sounds* poll. On 3rd March, Richard Attenborough, chairman of Capital Radio, presented Kate with the award for Best Female Vocalist of 1979 at the Grosvenor House Hotel in London. Tony Myatt, who was present at the ceremony recalls: 'It was a very exciting evening. I didn't know Kate was going to win anything, and when the results were announced I was really choking, because I thought if anybody deserved an award, Kate Bush deserved something. I was just so pleased for her. The funny thing was that everybody who got to know Kate at that particular time felt the same thing. It isn't just talent. She's just such a nice person. There's no "star tripping" with her.'

Continuing with the final remixing of the album, and working on the accompanying video presentations, Kate filmed 'Babooshka' and 'Delius' for a Dr Hook Special to be screened on BBC TV the following month. A few days later the album was complete.

'Breathing' was the first single to be released from the album, and on 11th April it received its world debut on BBC Radio 1's review programme. 'Breathing' is a highly stylistic portrait of a baby struggling for breath in the womb of its mother, caught in a world immediately following a nuclear holocaust. With its haunting rhythmic chant of '*Breathing, breathing my mother in*' the song is an incredible feat of lyric and melody. Kate, in an interview with *Zig Zag*, referred to 'Breathing' as her 'little symphony', the best thing she had written so far. Roy Harper sang in the resounding chorus of '*Leave us something to breathe*'. She attributes the inspiration for 'Breathing', to Pink Floyd and *The Wall*, saying that the 'vibe' of their album, their 'atomic' instrumentation, gave her the feeling for 'Breathing'. Kate puts the listener in the position of a very small foetus struggling between the will to live and the horror of being born into a frightening, poison-filled world. The video for the track has Kate encased in a plastic bubble signifying the placenta, rolling around in a womb-like set. There is also a scene showing quite explicitly a mushroom-clouded nuclear explosion which the BBC refused to air on 'Top of the Pops'.

The album was finally finished on 10th May. Its release was postponed for three months, however, because of other releases scheduled for the time, primarily a McCartney track 'Waterfalls' that would attract a lot of attention. In keeping with the promotional strategy for their protegée, EMI insisted upon a media event centred solely on Kate with no competing albums to dilute the glory. Kate took the time to relax and start to formulate ideas for her next album.

'Babooshka' was the next single to be released. It was a smash success, the first of her repertoire to come close to her initial hit, 'Wuthering Heights'. 'Babooshka' tells the story of a woman disguising herself as an alluring stranger, trying to gain the attention of her husband. A spectacular drama of love, suspicion and infidelity, the song calls upon her folk music tradition, borrowing from the Irish folk song 'Sovay Sovay' in her lyrics and enlisting the aid of Paddy's Balalaika. 'Babooshka' instantly caught on. Her sensual video emphasizes her curvy charm and sensuality, as she struts and grinds her way around a double bass, leering and moving with such overt sexual abandon that the BBC struggled to prohibit its airing.

Again Kate was caught in the struggle to preserve her image as a serious musician in the face of another very sexually-orientated album. 'Infant Kiss', a song with strong allusions to the 'unnatural' thoughts a mother has for her child on seeing the man behind his eyes, threw Kate back into the controversy that arose with 'The Kick Inside' and its incestuous theme. Kate clamoured to clear up what she considered a misinterpretation. In an interview with Harry Doherty of *Melody Maker* she notes that it was based on a film, *The Innocents*, which was in turn based on Henry James's short story, *The Turn of the Screw*, which tells of a governess looking after two children who are possessed with the spirits of the occupants who preceeded them in their home. She says: 'Some people might think it's a song about . . . what's the word when older women fancy little boys? It would worry me if people mixed it up with that because that's exactly what worries *her* so much. I find that distortion very fascinating and quite sad . . . I'm not actually thinking of myself falling in love with a little boy; I was putting myself in her place. I love children, and suddenly seeing something in their eyes that you don't want to see . . . It's like when a tiny kid turns around and says to you "You're a bastard".' Whatever the explanation, Kate Bush certainly leaves much to the imagination with lines like, '*But things are not right –/What is this? an infant kiss/That sends my body tingling'* and later, '*All my barriers are going*'. It is a distinct juxtaposition of unmotherly, unnatural feelings and maternal love that Kate is describing, and it doesn't quite fit her description of how she sees it.

'Delius' and 'Night Scented Stock' are less vibrant and vivid, calling heavily on what Kate calls 'auras'. They become rather weak versions of the ballad formula that she perfected in the first two albums. 'Delius' did, however, meet the approval of Eric Fenby, who called it 'a very gracious tribute' to his mentor Frederick Delius on the BBC TV chat show 'Russell Harty'.

'The Wedding List' alternates between a whimsical, lonely soft-pitched voice and a wavering, demanding deep thrust in the chorus, and was inspired by a Jeanne Moreau film in which a bride's husband was killed and she sought revenge from the murderers. There is a strong male back-up and the same sort of circus-like rhythm that characterized 'Coffee Homeground' from *Lionheart*. The track has been likened to Steely Dan, although its subject matter is a unique and highly orchestrated imitation of the medieval ballad form.

The third single to be released from the album was 'Army Dreamers', which takes a terrifying and raw look at the emotions of a mother whose son has been killed in battle: the regret, the reminiscing, the feeling of waste, wondering what he could have become. Kate uses her voice to its extreme in a lilting falsetto, at once childish and painful. The bewildered 'little girl' vocals contrast sharply with the lyrics in a delightfully stark irony. She says, 'It's not specifically about Ireland, it's just putting the case of the mother in these circumstances, how incredibly sad it is for her. How she feels she should have been able to prevent it.' The video itself is a masterpiece of dance and illusion and it warranted much critical acclaim. Clad in camouflage, traditional army wear, Kate reaches for a child that constantly eludes her grasp, while a mandolin lilts over the track of a regimentary style drill.

In September 1980, Kate promoted the album in Germany, performing an altered version of 'Army Dreamers' in which she appears bedecked in a washer-woman's garb, complete with mop. She dances her way around four uniformed soldiers, ending the number spread protectively over their hunched backs. The song charted in October of that year and soon hit the number 16 position.

The official release of *Never For Ever* took place on 8th September and on 16th September the album officially entered the charts in the number 1 position. Kate Bush was the first woman in music history to have a number one solo album. 'Babooshka' remained the most successful single of the album, reaching number 5 where it stayed for several weeks. 'Breathing' also managed to fit into the charts at 16. She'd done it again.

Having taken every opportunity to dismiss Kate Bush as a weird, one-hit wonder in spite of her unmistakeable popular appeal, the critics were mystified. Her unusual lyrics and unique vocals continued to capture the attention of the Press worldwide, attracting hundreds of thousands of fans in her meteoric rise to stardom. She was touted as the sex princess of the 80s, a label which refused to phase her. She said, in her defence, 'Sex is a fascinating subject, it's so beautiful in so many ways and some of my songs intentionally reflect that. But not all my songs are meant to be sexual. Other people may interpret them that way and it may be subconscious on my part. Music to me is very much like making love.'

Astounding. With the innocent demeanour of a fifteen-year-old, and the cherub-like face of an elf, Kate Bush had reached new heights of sexuality in music and got away with it. Never crass, never criticized, Kate Bush continued to find new forms of expression, shattering the traditional 'come up to the mike and sing' concept of the rock star. Her body, her voice, her lyrics and her astonishingly intelligent concepts and analysis made it clear that it was all very well planned. It was a manipulative promotion of herself and her music that stunned first a nation and then the world. At twenty-one years old, Kate Bush was the most talked about female musician in the world, selling more posters than sex symbol Debbie Harry and consistently taking over the music charts with her startling compositions. She had proved herself as an entrepreneur on the video form and a master of music style. And there was much much more to come.

7
DIVA

Won't letcha in for love nor money
My home is my joy and I'm barred and bolted and I
Won't letcha in

'Get Out of My House'
Kate Bush, 1982

Born Catherine, nicknamed Cathy and, as she grew up, called Kate.
Three names, how many personalities? Kate Bush has remained an
enigma in the music world, releasing titbits about herself every two
years or so, just enough to keep people hanging on. When Kate Bush
gives an interview, people listen. She's tight with her interviews,
doing a string of about six or seven every year and only when it is
convenient for her, certainly not when she is in a creative stint, which
is most of the time. It's difficult to decide whether Kate Bush is
frantically chased because she is so popular or popular because she is
so frantically chased. It is her mysteriousness that provokes so much
speculation. Critics and interviewers pamper her, argue at her,
insult her and end up with the same result every time – raised
eyebrows and empty notebooks. Sure she'll discuss her music, the
central focus of her life in which she seemingly has no other hobbies
or preferences – or any personal life for that matter. She is truly the
Greta Garbo of pop – she just wants to be alone. It is true that, she
has every reason to lead a private life outside the plastic bubble
that surrounds most pop starts, otherwise known as the goldfish
syndrome. But arguably, for someone who offers herself up so
extensively and intensely in her music, she is remarkably frugal with
the details of her life. Who is the real Kate Bush, the person inside
that sweet, charming elfin figure who holds the key to the British

pop scene in her tight little fist? She's so frustratingly elusive it's annoying. But the infuriating thing is that she is so incredibly polite. So incredibly naïve and so very very nice. Even those reviewers with hearts of granite cannot fail to be charmed by Kate Bush. She has everyone right where she wants them.

Kate Bush is ordinary enough physically. She is 5 foot 3½ inches tall, with the bone structure of a sparrow. She is much much tinier than her stage presence suggests. Her weight is generally about seven or eight stone, but she admits to having trouble keeping it down when she lets herself go. Without the regimen of exercise and a staunch vegetarian diet, she puts on weight easily. There were periods in her life where this was apparent. At the screening of *Brazil* in February 1985 Kate appeared noticeably heavier than normal, though she hadn't reached the eighteen stone that the critics suggested. It was the period immediately after *The Dreaming*, and Kate herself confirmed that she was extremely out of shape. With her delicate bone structure it is easy to see how a few pounds could make a big difference to her frame. There were further rumours when Kate appeared live at the Peter Gabriel concert at Earl's Court in London in June 1987: it was said that she was pregnant. Arriving on stage in baggy clothing to join Peter for 'Don't Give Up', Kate did look even heavier than on the previous occasion. At that time she was in the middle of recording her seventh album and attributed the weight gain, as she had before, to insufficient exercise.

Kate finds solace in exercise. She credited her new-found dance teacher Diane Gray with the energy that enabled her to create *Hounds of Love* after her two year disappearance from the music world. 'I found a really inspirational new dance teacher, one that had the energy to make me really enthusiastic about writing again . . . I love the discipline of dance.'

The Bush family owns a large Victorian house in Eltham, surrounded by eight-foot wrought iron gates. She has never lived there but it is here that she conducts interviews, away from her own home. Here she has an enormous dance studio with mirrored walls and a large window overlooking the Blackheath Golf Course which lets in a great deal of sun. Two velvet cushions, a double-bass and an unusual picture (one of Kate's favourites) of a doll lying on its side in a pool of water with a cracked skull are the only items that adorn the otherwise bare white walls. Kate also enjoys riding a bicycle, a hobby that she shares with lover Del Palmer. Otherwise, any exercise that she gets is in the form of the movement that accompanies her music. Kate Bush writes her songs with a strong visual aspect in mind. She finds music most complete when it is expressed physically as well as verbally.

Kate Bush loves chocolate, and many of the musicians who have worked with her state that she swears by it to get her through the long studio sessions. Stuart Elliot remembers: 'I think a lot of people expect a Kate Bush session to be shrouded in mystery – you know, she's a kind of mysterious character. There certainly is a chocolate element to Kate's sessions – she is a sucker for the chocolate. On a lot of sessions she actually lived on chocolate. I don't know how she did it, I can't understand it.' Swiss chocolate is a particular favourite of Kate's, although when she appeared at the Virgin record store to promote *The Dreaming* she came armed with three Cadbury's Caramels for the four-hour session.

Kate is a very devoted vegetarian, claiming that she originally became so quite suddenly. 'Mum had made a stew and as I was eating it, chewing and grinding away at the muscle fibres, I suddenly started to realize that it was a dead animal I was eating and I just couldn't eat meat from then on'. Kate felt so strongly about it that two years after becoming a vegetarian she wrote an article for *Woman's World* entitled 'How Can You Eat Dead Animals'. Kate likes to cook and has moved on from the cheese and nut cutlets that were her staple diet upon first giving up meat. 'I like to experiment, there are so many different kinds of vegetables and I am just learning how to prepare them all.' Kate bakes her own bread 'when I have time, but it is something I really do enjoy'. And she does her own washing up claiming that it keeps her feet on the ground. 'I make myself do things like scrub out the bath, just to keep in touch with things.' She also claims she cannot work with a sink of washing up to do, a need for cleanliness having been instilled in her at an early age.

Kate doesn't drink much coffee, preferring tea. The Bush family is noted for the amount of tea they drink: most of her musicians remember there being buckets of tea and biscuits and Kit Kats about during every session. She doesn't drink much alochol, claiming that it disagrees with her constitution. 'I don't really like alcohol, it doesn't get on with my body . . . I've got a great stomach for food though.' She has been pictured, however, with drink in hand. On most occasions it is red wine or champagne. On the question of drugs Kate denies taking them, claiming that she never took them as a teenager, and therefore there would be no need to start them at a later stage. She finds her own 'high' in her imagination and natural stimuli – nature, films, love. There are several people who are convinced that Kate does some drugs, but there are, however, so many conflicting reports floating about that it is impossible to discern between reality and supposition. When pressed an EMI executive simply stated that he didn't know what Kate did on her own, his business was her records.

Kate's hair is professionally cut and styled by the renowned Anthony Yacomine at the John Freida Salon in London. He is also responsible for the coiffures of such clients as the Duchess of Gloucester and Selina Scott. Kate credits him with the design and production of the boyish wig she wore in the video 'Cloudbusting', noting, 'The credit actually belongs to my hairdresser Anthony, he did a brilliant job, it looked so real.' Kate has kept her hair long throughout her career because of the different looks and styles she is able to achieve with it. However, she says: 'I have considered cutting my hair, it's something I've just got to do one day, really. I just like to grow it long, it's such a useful vehicle for visuals, having long hair, there's such a lot of things you can do with it, but yes I'd like to cut it some day. For the video I found short hair portrayed a much stronger look of innocence, which was necessary for the role I was playing.' She frequently tints her hair with a pinky-auburn rinse that picks up the natural red highlights that run through her tousled mop.

Kate prefers wearing comfortable clothes – jeans, sweatshirts, T-shirts and going barefoot. She borrows jumpers from her boyfriend and likes oversized garments. Kate shops in antique clothes markets – when she has time – but otherwise, anywhere will do: Soho, Covent Garden and the King's Road in London. She usually wears heels because of her height, preferring boots to shoes. Her clothes aside from performances are never extraordinary, reflecting perhaps the simple life that seems to agree with her. She states firmly that she is not a 'victim to fashion'. Kate does prefer simplicity in her appearance, wearing very little make up – just a bit of grey contour around her amber eyes – and a touch of lipstick. On stage, however, and in her promotional videos, she likes to experiment with different looks, using a variety of cosmetics to enhance an image.

Kate Bush smokes a great deal and expresses concern about it. She rolls her own cigarettes and although she has made attempts to kick the habit has not been successful so far. Her voice does not appear to be affected. Both her brothers also smoke. She draws the line at smoking in public, declaring it an unattractive habit, and has somehow always managed to avoid being photographed with cigarette in hand.

Her hobbies centre mainly around music – things that can be drawn upon for songs. She reads a great deal, her favourite authors being Kurt Vonnegut, CS Lewis, Emily Brontë, Stephen King, Henry James and of course Peter Reich. Although she is not under his influence, as the extraordinary Vermorel biography suggested, Kate enjoys reading Gurdjieff, the Russian mystic occultist. Her family shares her interest in mythology – Greek, Roman and Anglo Saxon.

She was brought up Roman Catholic, but feels it was too restrictive; an agnostic by nature, she believes in 'the forces and energies that humans and other things which are alive can create. I do feel that what you give out sincerely then karmically you should get back.' She's got an answer for everything.

Her brothers are both very literate, passing on their books to Kate. She claims she is a slow reader and when she began writing songs found it difficult to make the time. She said, 'I think whenever I have the time to read I am always inspired by it. The problem is that I just shun it in that I feel there are more important things to do with my time – which is rubbish really – but I do feel guilty when I sit down and read a book because I know I should be doing other things. It takes me such a long time to read. But in a way, there is no other experience like it – the intimate relationship between yourself and a book is incredible, and it's very sad that things like television and films – although it's great because they are encouraging books by using their scripts for films – take away from that whole world of books. But I think particularly films do inspire me. I've always had a television. I used to watch lots and lots of television when I was a kid and I really enjoy watching films.'

Several of Kate's tracks have been inspired by films; the Ninth Wave conceptual side to *Hounds of Love* was inspired by war films, as she noted herself; 'The imagery came from war movies, old war movies, where men come out into the water, little groups of them, an incredibly desolate set of human beings in that great expanse of water.' 'Hammer Horror' was inspired by a Cagney flick; 'Hello Earth' by Nosferatu; and, 'The Wedding List' by a Jeanne Moreau film. She watches a lot of television, and has one in her kitchen at home. She declares that she'll watch almost anything, from 'Breakfast TV' to 'Dynasty', but she particularly likes old movies. 'I do tend to watch a lot of rubbish on TV but it's just to keep in touch with what is going on . . . when I'm working. I get up, go to the studio, work there all day then come home and go to bed. There's just no time to take anything in. I live an isolated lifestyle. It's hard to keep up.'

Kate prefers classical music to pop, although she expressed a great deal of interest in the latest cult of New Wave artists. She has some old favourites like Bowie, Killing Joke, Steely Dan, early Boomtown Rats and claims to admire the Sex Pistols, although she doesn't quite approve of the violence. A sixties child by heart, she appreciates the Beatles, but finds most inspiration in Billie Holliday ('She was so soulful'), Gene Kelly and Judy Garland. 'As a kid the idea of being a star was attractive as I think it is to every child,' comments Kate. 'They love things that are larger than life, and dreams and fantasies, but most children never grow out of it to the day they die. I think I didn't ever consider the idea of actually being a so-called famous songwriter/singer. I think as a very young child I aspired to being something like a great acress. I was very enamoured by people like Judy Garland – I thought she was incredible, so beautiful.' She doesn't listen to much popular music and in fact when asked what the last album she purchased was, claimed that she couldn't honestly remember. Lotte Lenya influenced her, and so did Weill and Brecht. Bach remains a favourite as well as the traditional folk music, European, Irish and British, that her family takes so much delight in.

Other hobbies include archery and dance, both of which have been incorporated to a certain degree in her music. She enjoys cooking and as Simon Drake, the illusionist who worked with Kate on her live tour, noted: 'The whole family is really into nature. I mean they will all stand at a window for ages to watch a sunset or to watch the wind in the trees.' Kate herself has mentioned that nature is a great stimulus for her – that her most pleasant pastime is communing with nature, although she firmly states that that doesn't mean 'hugging trees at 3am'. All of her households, except her Brockley flat, were surrounded to a degree by uncontrolled wilderness, and she found herself suffocating in the cement confines of London. 'You can't really *breathe* in the city.' she once said.

Kate loves animals, which is probably one of the factors that led to her eventual vegetarianism. She has had numerous pets in the past – rabbits, hamsters, the family dog, Piggy – making pets of the numerous wild animals in her garden, mainly squirrels and birds. She had two cats, Zoodle and Pyewacket, who have been transported from home to home as she has moved; when Zoodle died in early 1987, Kate adopted three kittens: Sparky, Torchy and Rocket. She also feels very strongly about the killing of whales and seals. 'I hate the idea of unnecessary slaughter of whales and seals when we don't really need the products from them.' She doesn't wear fur coats, but succumbs to leather boots and accessories – necessities, she says. In aid of Greenpeace, she offered 'Breathing' for their album *Greenpeace* in the UK and the USA.

Kate likes to collect earrings, although she says she doesn't actually have that many, having very little time for shopping in general. Her favourite collection consists of letters from friends, which she says she cherishes, keeping them in a box and rereading them frequently. Kate has a number of friends. Her good friend Lisa Bradley, with whom she attended school, is now on the Bush payroll running the official fan club, The Kate Bush Club. Jon Kelly, the engineer on her early albums, remembers: 'Kate was very open about her life to her friends. She'd have long chats with people, she'd love to sit and chat away. She'd have a group of friends that would turn up to watch the recording, people she wanted there. I think she insisted upon privacy from people she didn't want there, but if it was a friend, people she knew, then it was fine. They weren't there to criticize, they would just pass quiet comments. She invited her friends into the studio for moral support. She was a friendly, gregarious person and I think she likes the people she knows well to be around her. During the third album I can remember people would often come in the evenings. Personal friends . . . there would always be someone there every evening.'

Andrew Powell, her producer, remembers that she liked to chat. 'Sometimes we'd get off into long tangential conversations about subject matters of songs. I remember one particular one was the song on the first album called 'Strange Phenomena' which was basically about what Jung would call synchronicity, where you suddenly think about somebody one day who you haven't seen for ten years and walk into him the next day. I remember that one went on for absolutely hours. Most of them were actually related to what we were doing in some vague way.' Kate became literally gleeful if she discovered common ground with one of her colleagues. Simon Drake recalls: 'I can remember at the first meeting we had certain things in common which Kate would probably call synchronicities. Both of us had fathers who were doctors and our brothers were at the same college: my brother was at the London School of Furniture Design and Paddy was there as well studying ancient musical instruments. So we had these things that were in common and once she saw what I was doing with floating objects, dance, mime, magic and so on, it became fairly clear that we would do something. She's very interested in, how would you put it . . . not the occult in terms of anything dark, but that sort of area – the unexplained. Obviously I can't speak for her, but basically things that were in that sort of sphere. You can hear this on the first album, there are a lot of references to Gurdjieff and that type of mysticism, an experimental sort of mysticism, Gurdjieff being a Russian philosopher who had theories about dancing and freeing the spirit and finding yourself . . . I suppose I had a similar set of interests to those of Kate and we hit it off immediately.'

Her disposition is a perpetually pleasant one: not one of her friends or colleagues can ever remember her raising her voice. She remains even-tempered in all situations, and in the light of her extraordinary success and subsequent fame, it is astonishing that none of its trappings have affected her in the least. Jon Kelly comments, 'She didn't change much. Only in the respect that maybe she lost some of her naïvety from the original days, but that would have happened anyway, in anybody's progression of their career. I think Kate has always stayed as much as she can the way she is. I think she's shunned the personal success a little. I think she likes to stay her own character and her own personality. She didn't become nasty in any respect. Without a doubt, her success did not go to her head and make her conceited or arrogant in any way. She is still the same.' Kate herself has strong views on the expression of anger. 'I don't think I'm actually an aggressive person. I think I can be . . . but I release that energy in work. I think it's wrong to get angry. If people get angry, it kind of freaks everybody out and they can't concentrate on what they are doing.'

She jealously guards her privacy, and honestly cannot understand why people would be interested in her private life, or for that matter why they would want an autograph. 'I think the public have been conditioned to want to know who is sleeping with who or how many marriages someone has had, but as far as I'm concerned, it's totally irrelevant. I'm really very normal and there is nothing sensational to uncover. There was a time when I thought of myself as a bit of a freak. I really got paranoid at one point. People wanted to stare and touch. I still feel self-conscious when I sign autographs. I've never been too interested in fame . . . fame isn't even my ambition. I want to carry on learning, getting more information, creating and realizing ideas.'

Kate looks pleased when her music is described as being weird. 'EMI are quite happy to let me be a bit weird because they haven't got that many weirdos on the label.' She goes on to say, 'I try to cultivate a sort of weirdness,' although she becomes increasingly distressed at having constantly to explain the rationale behind her songs. 'I guess it's a lot to expect people to actually sit down and read my lyrics, but I really don't know why people consider my songs all that strange.' The weirdness that Kate says she cultivates must be in her own mind visually or vocally, because she seems to consider her lyrics straightforward.

Kate Bush is very much an eighties woman, managing her life, career and finances herself with the help of her family. Kate can be slightly disorganized when looking after her own affairs. Jon Kelly remembers: 'Always late. Every day she was late, but never because she was lazy or didn't care. It was because she was a little bit absent-minded and time would slip away from her very very quickly. I would never ask her for an excuse – not that she ever had to give one. It was part of her character because when she got there it was all right and you could carry on working.'

Kate feels strongly on a number of current issues, atomic energy, the plight of the aborigines and feminism coming most easily to mind. She claims that she is not a feminist as such, that she believes in her own strengths and the strengths of women, but does need someone – a man – to be there for her. When asked by *Daily Express* journalist David Wigg if she felt the sexual attraction of women was a handicap, she strongly ascertained, 'It's how you use it. Women who feel they don't have it are just as worried. Women have a tremendous advantage if they use their attraction properly, but I think it's a good thing not to be aware of it. Otherwise, it's not healthy. I think we get far too worried about what our hair looks like and what kind of shoes we are wearing instead of just loving life.' Later she noted,' I think when I first appeared it was incredibly unusual for a young female to be writing her own songs . . . many people latched on to the physical side of me. I was flattered, and it did help me to establish my music'. She thrives on love, as was indicated by her peaceful sojourn with boyfriend Del following *The Dreaming* flop.

Del Palmer took over after her relationship with childhood sweetheart Al Buckle, and there has been no looking back. In the early stages of her career, when she was less open about her personal life, she claimed to have not one but many boyfriends, but said she found herself too busy to spend time with men. 'I think a lot of men are frightened by me and intimidated. That's why the men I like best have to be strong. In purpose and in mind. I'm a very romantic person.' She went on to say, 'I think men are really great, but I'm really in love with my music – always have been and always will. That's the strong involvement in my life and it would take someone really patient to fit into that. When I work I have to be alone. I can live on my own, but it's much nicer to have someone there to share things with.'

After *The Dreaming*, and subsequently *Hounds of Love*, Kate became much more open about her relationship with Del, crediting him with an influence on *Hounds*, and for generally helping her to pick up the pieces of her life after running herself down to such a degree. 'I have a very good, strong relationship with Del. We are not man and wife, but we are two people who love one another and work well together.'

80

In an interview with Mike Nicholls of *The Times*, she enthusiastically pulled out an antique pocket watch that Del had presented her with for her twenty-seventh birthday, gushing: 'It gives off really old vibes! I can almost imagine being taken back to the time it was made.'

Kate has lived with Del since 1978, and enjoys the homey aspects of their life together, growing vegetables, watching television and just cuddling. She still finds her career much the most important thing to her at this stage, and hasn't any immediate plans to start a family, although she does confess to having maternal instincts every now and then. 'I really am totally obsessed by my work . . . it would take a strong urge to persuade me to have babies.' She feels at this stage of her career that her albums are surrogate children and are certainly as time-consuming. She did state that she would give up her career were she to have children. She feels very strongly that, as her mother did, she would stay at home. It is something she looks forward to.

Del, despite the fact that he works with Kate, shares very little of the limelight, but it does not distress him. In an interview with John Blake of the *Daily Mirror*, he said: 'I never worry about the fact that she is famous. For me there are two Kates. There is the girl at home I love and there is Kate the star. I must admit that I sometimes wonder what she sees in me, but it's not something I worry about too much.' Kate also sees herself as two people, and makes certain that she separates Kate the star from the person she is at home. She says, 'Sometimes I see myself in the paper and it's hard to associate with the name Kate Bush . . . I'm just working on my music'.

She likes an intelligent man, finding that a far more attractive quality than physical appearance. She adds: 'I think a body is really nice – but it doesn't last forever, does it?' Sex is a subject that a number of her songs dwell upon, and she eagerly professes to enjoy it. She finds music and making love very similar, as music is to love in general (a theme prominent on every album): 'The communication of music is very much like making love. If you play the piano, for example, you're so united it's really a beautiful thing.' She does not tend to discuss her sexual life in any further detail, saying: 'I want to keep my private life private. It's a sanctuary.' The eroticism of Kate Bush is undeniable, however, and no virgin, even one as imaginative as Kate, could write a song like 'Feel It', or 'L'Amour Looks Something Like You'.

Kate is afraid of flying. She is slightly miffed, however, when the subject is brought up, hotly denying that she is afraid, but rather explaining that it just isn't her favourite manner in which to travel: 'I think people have got the impression that I am carried on to a plane screaming, at the moment, and have to be knocked out so that I can cope with the journey. I don't like flying, but it's really not that bad, and I do fly if I have to. If there is another way of travelling, I quite often prefer to go that way; but if you have to fly and it's the quickest way to get somewhere, then I do.'

Dreams are something which Kate Bush can avidly discuss. Over the last decade she has had a series of extremely unusual dreams, ones that she thinks have some sort of meaning. She purports that visits to her in her dreams by Peter O'Toole and Keith Moon helped her to write some of the more sensual tracks on *The Hounds Of Love*. She notes, 'I have very strange dreams. Very famous people come to visit me . . . they are very helpful to me when I am writing my songs.' In her dreams these famous people stop by to have tea and meet Kate's Mum. She claims that heroes like Hitchcock, Oscar Wilde, Roxy Music and Billie Holiday have had a part in these vivid dreams, and that she carries their influence over into her music. This particular phenomenon sheds some light on her oft-discussed inspiration.

Dreams are very important to Kate, as was revealed on 'The Ninth Wave', where the dreamlike, hallucinogenic state that her central character moves through is the key to his self-discovery. In *The Secret Life Of Kate Bush* Fred Vermorel claims that Kate's mother also had odd dreams, once hovering on the edge of death for a few moments. In the book, Kate recounts; 'When I was little my mother fainted for no apparent reason. My father was there and put her on the bed, but he couldn't feel any pulse so he started doing artificial respiration and so on to revive her. Meanwhile, according to my mum, she'd taken off like a balloon and hit the ceiling. She was looking down from there at my father pushing her body about and she was calling out "Leave me alone, I'm all right!". Then I walked in asking, "Where's my Mum" and when she saw me she dropped down into her body, she says. Anyway she did come back to life.'

If this is an accurate story, it is not difficult to understand where

Kate inherited her exaggerated imagination from. With such intense and obscure stimuli surrounding her, it is no wonder that she required an outlet, in her case, music.

Kate Bush is an unusual and highly emotional young lady who has successfully conquered the need to talk about herself by putting her fears, thoughts and ideals into music. Even then she remains obscure, her lyrics coded with memories and unintelligible experiences. She is a truly likeable woman, with a high, consonantless-sounding mode of speech betraying a cross between a suburban South London accent and some sort of contrived innocence.

Kate remains as cordial as she was in 1978 when she first broke into the scene, but has revealed very little about herself since that date. It is only fair to respect her need for privacy, although there are those that say there is nothing at all beneath her cool and kind demeanour. She lives within the complex world of her music – anything and everything that surrounds her is drawn into its enigmatic depths. She lives for her music and she breathes anything that affects it. Her friends are generally involved in her music to some degree; when she isn't writing she just doesn't enjoy going out. She dislikes discos, nightclubs and claims that aside from the odd Indian meal, she does not go to restaurants unless taken to one by her record company. She becomes ill at the sight of meat – and feels very strongly about her vegetarianism. Simon Drake recalls that she didn't speak to him for weeks after he inadvertently ordered a lobster at the same table. She apparently blanched at the sight of it. Her political views are not abnormal and she watches a lot of television to keep up on current events. She supports causes like the Third World famine and Amnesty, and doesn't feel any need for chemicals to keep her high. She seems to be just a little too good to be true. But how can you knock that?

8
THE PLAYERS

They'll get nothing from me
Not until they let me see
My solicitor
'There Goes a Tenner'
Kate Bush, 1982

The management of Kate Bush was taken over at an early stage in her career by her family and, to a certain extent, by Kate herself. She felt very strongly that any decisions made should be either her own or those of the people that she had trusted throughout her life. Because she was so very young, and because EMI had already realized that there would be some parental involvement, they were more than willing to allow the decision-making to be taken out of their hands. Hilary Walker, who was working in the public relations department of EMI when Kate was signed, became a friend of Kate's after 'Wuthering Heights'. The success of Kate's first track was partly attributed to Hilary's hard work – her finesse in dealing with the networking of the track and its video – and the Bush family therefore hired Hilary as agent to look after Kate's affairs. Hilary remains her agent to this day and is well known in the music world for her professionalism and her sturdy support of Kate under any circumstances.

Hilary Walker deals with all aspects of Kate's career: the promotion of her videos, the organization of tours and personal appearances, the day-to-day dealings with the Press and radio industry. She remains a personal friend and buffer to Kate, protecting her from all the less salubrious aspects of her success. It was Hilary Walker who firmly supported Kate's decision to prepare herself more fully for a recording career by taking several years off after signing with EMI. Hilary confirms: 'If you're thinking in terms of longevity for a pop singer, rather than the instant-fame-and-gone-tomorrow approach, then that artist really needs to keep on growing inside.' She felt that Kate had the natural talent to become something special, noting, 'Her songs and her vocal presentation were fresh and different to a degree I'd not come across for three or four years.' Leaving an excellent job at EMI behind, Hilary took it into her own hands to ensure that Kate was well managed.

Kate had always been something of a child wonder, even in the Bush household, being the youngest child and certainly the most obviously gifted. The supportive unit that had cared for her in her childhood now stood behind her in her career, protecting her and making sure that she was able to work creatively without having to bear the strain of any unnecessary administrative decisions. Kate has always been looked upon as the baby of the pop world – and thanks to her family encasing her so successfully in a protective bubble, that image has continued to thrive even into her adult years.

Before the public became aware of Kate's need to be able to depend on someone for these sorts of decisions, the involvement of the family was looked upon as unnatural and even incestuous to a degree. Speculation was that they were living on the success of EMI's protegée and that she had lost control of her whole life, not just the musical aspect, to those who surrounded her. Kate, however, disputes any such theories: 'I've always had an attitude about managers. Unless they are really needed they just confuse matters. They obviously have their own impressions of a direction and an image that is theirs, and surely it should come from within the actual structure rather than from outside. I often think that generally they're more of a hindrance than a help'.

Kate has always been concerned with her image, declaring early in her career that she did not want to be promoted as a singles chart sex symbol, but rather as a serious artist – one who had honed her talents to be justifiably as deserving of critical attention as any male artist. She even went to the point of noting that she did not see herself as a woman at the piano, rather more of an asexual creature – a 'spirit'. 'I like to think I'm writing not as a human being but as a spirit. I tend to write songs from the male angle. But I wouldn't like to have been born male . . . I'm very happy to be female.' She attributed the original descriptions of her as 'weird' or 'sexy' to the fact that she was a woman, and that there were very few female solo artists currently on the scene. 'When I was first happening, the only other female on the level I was being promoted at was Blondie. We were both being promoted on the basis of being female bodies as well as singers. I wasn't looked at as being a female singer/songwriter. People were not even generally aware that I wrote my own songs or played the piano until maybe a year or so after that. The media just promoted me as a female body. It's like I have had to prove that I'm an artist inside a female body. The idea of the body as a vehicle is . . . just one of those things.'

Feeling confident that her family was aware of her talents and were not likely to exploit her body as a means of promotion, Kate felt it was befitting that they should oversee her career. Initially they set up a holding company, Novercia Holdings Limited, under which Kate Bush Music, Novercia Limited, Novercia Overseas Limited, Kate Bush Music Overseas Limited and Techgrove Limited eventually fell. Records show that each member of the Bush family, Patrick John Carder, Dr John, Kate and Hannah are all directors, with Kate's mother even acting in some cases as company secretary.

Kate is managing director, although she and her family are agreed that most decisions do not require her complete involvement. Kate does not have the time to become involved to any great degree in financial matters. 'If I actually start thinking about that side of it, it just freaks me out so much it starts affecting my work to the point of almost stopping me wanting to write. So I just don't think about it. I never think of myself as being in the middle of a vast business set-up. Everyone that I work with is very much into the vibe, if you like of what's happening. They're much more interested in the artistic side than the making money and being successful side, and as long as the whole feeling is concentrated on that rather than on business priorities, then everything will be OK.'

Kate does demand a certain amount of control over the marketing and promotion of her product. She has been firm on a number of occasions with EMI, stating quite distinctly who and what she wants to be seen as, and therefore how. She notes: 'I am my own boss – that's so important to me. I don't find it hard to be strong. There are a lot of things that come up that I have to fight against not doing. Once you've stated your point strongly enough, people usually understand.' It is the degree of comfort she finds in maintaining some control over her destiny that allows Kate the freedom to create without the pressures of the business overtaking her. 'I think I'm pretty stable, though I have people around me who are very good to be with. It's important to realize that your career can never be your whole life.'

John Bush, Kate's eldest brother, trained in law and was a writer before taking on both the general legalities of Kate's career and the smooth running of the companies that were incorporated for her. He feels very strongly that Kate is well taken care of, and is known as being a great comfort to Kate. He has since taken on the bulk of her photography, thus eliminating such outrageously sexual poses as those that personified the early EMI-style promotion. The rights for most of Kate's pictures, both video stills and record sleeve/promotional portraits, remain in the family and will not be released under any circumstances. John Bush is in the process of preparing a biographical study of Kate using his own pictures. The first of the collection, entitled simply *Cathy*, was published privately in 1986 and was available only in a limited quantity through mail order. The family are able to control to a certain degree any publications concerning Kate and ensure that her career is recorded with complete integrity.

Paddy Bush has become a recognizable character in the backing band and is also responsible for a large number of her more unusual instrumental tracks. She feels strongly that his influence on her music and his part in both vocals and instrumentation is limitless. Kate's music has become his career, and an outlet for his creativity which at one time took the form of poetry. Kate has always worked with Paddy musically, from the first time she played piano to his violin. Paddy liaises with the Kate Bush Club, Kate's official fan club, keeping them up to date on her activities and organizing personal appearances with her fans.

The family is concerned that Kate's wish to maintain an insulated private life is kept up. They are, in general, opposed to personal interviews and remain as modest as Kate in not recognizing the public interest in them. Kate does not, in all honesty, understand why people should be interested in her life. She feels that she is fulfilling something in people's lives through her music and therefore sees no need to offer what remains her only privacy to others. Her modesty is admirable, but it remains baffling in the sense that there are very few artists who are so high-profile and who continue to refuse to offer that little bit greater understanding of the person behind the music.

Financially, Kate has been incredibly successful, illustrating that her management has been wise and frugal. Of the original three hundred shares which made up Novercia Holdings Limited, Kate holds 240 and Paddy and Jay 30 each. In 1981, two years after the company was formed, the shares were drawn up to include Kate Bush Music Limited, Novercia Limited and Novercia Overseas Limited. Shares allotted reached 900, with 800 going to Kate and 100 to her brothers. Dr Bush and Mrs Bush remained directors, but were not shareholders. From 1981 to 1986, Kate's holding company showed a net revenue of the following amounts: 1981: £418,953; 1982: £561,400; 1983: £586,418; 1984: £517,192; 1985: £444,878; 1986: £686,954. Turnover for 1986 was £1,501,822 with a profit of £809,851 before taxation. It is interesting to note that the directors of the holding company along with Kate's own company staff members make up the bulk of her liability. A great deal of money has been set aside each year for pensions, ensuring that when Kate does give up her musical career both she and her family will be well taken care of. In 1986, two of the directors (unnamed) of Novercia Holding Company were remunerated to the extent of £70,001–£75,000. The highest paid director of that year, in all likelihood Kate, was paid £144,000. The family are paid director's fees for the four other companies in which they sit on the board. Thus it appears that there is no lack of money, and that it is kept safely within the confines of the Bush family.

Kate has done very well financially, with assets of well over a million pounds sterling, and substantial investments and personal pension plans kept aside from the business. She has noted on a number of occasions that she will not continue to write forever; that after each album she feels a need to reassess the situation, and make decisions for the next few years of her life. After *Hounds Of Love*, Kate noted: 'I do know that I want to continue making albums, but in a way it's the gaps between albums that say what's going to happen next. I don't know what I'll be doing next. There's a choice of two or three things, so I'm just ploughing through the promotion at the end of this year and then next year I'll sit down and think what's next.'

Because of the theatrics that have been incorporated into Kate's music and the success of her 'Cloudbusting' video, acting seemed a natural step to take. She had been offered a number of roles in various films, specifically horror films after 'Hammer Horror' and 'Wuthering Heights', but she does not feel that that would be the correct vehicle for her talents. In a Canadian interview she noted: 'I've been offered a lot of really good roles with respected directors that I have had to turn down because of the time factor with my music. I have such commitments. I hope I get some nice offers – superb – like that again, and at a time that I can handle doing it.'

She noted on another occasion that perhaps her talents were more suited to direction. 'There's no doubt that if I was offered a part by a director who I really admired then I'm sure I would do it, but it doesn't actually interest me in terms of giving up music to take up a career in acting – it doesn't attract me at all – but I would certainly do it if it was one of my favourite directors, and most certainly if Donald Sutherland was in it. I'm not sure what role I would like to play. I certainly wouldn't want to play the part of a rock singer or a pop singer. I would be doing it as a challenge of the acting. If the part was something that I felt that I could convey well, then I'd certainly be up for trying it. It's fascinating – the whole process of making films; of suddenly becoming someone; showing feelings that you haven't been feeling five minutes before. The whole process is extraordinary and fascinating. I sometimes have to sit and listen to all these voices that are in me that seem to want to do too many different things sometimes. I really do like the idea of directing, but I don't think it's practical for me to direct and be in something, and while I'm actually performing visually, I would also very much like to work with a director because I think it's just too difficult to do it all. But the idea of directing is far in the future at the moment. It is much more attractive than performing in front of a camera.'

Kate has turned down a number of roles, including the lead in Lucy Irvine's *Castaway*, for which she finally ended up offering a track for the soundtrack, 'Be Kind To My Mistakes'. There were also a number of rumours that when Sarah Brightman left the London showing of *Phantom of the Opera*, Kate was offered her position. Because of the pressures of recording her sixth album, Kate declined.

Kate was commended for her, albeit short, acting role in the seven-minute 'Cloudbusting' video and was certainly held in high esteem by Donald Sutherland, who remarked that he would be delighted to work with Kate again. With Kate being a woman of so many talents, it was not difficult to understand why her family are so protective of her. She has been proudly guarded since her entrance into the music world; the lives of her entire family were irrevocably changed because of her. In his book, *Cathy*, John Carder Bush notes: 'Much has changed since these photographs were taken, some twenty years ago, and we in her family have changed. The sudden introduction of fame into a human unit forces decision and action, and they change people.' Kate Bush was and is something special, a fact which her family recognized at an early stage. She has always been taken care of, has been the shimmering light around which her family and friends have focused their lives. Her family and, in turn, her business have commandeered themselves into a circular front, within which she is zealously defended.

Kate has affected not only her family and friends but also numerous other musicians with her unusual style and imaginative self-expression. The Eurythmics, for example, have adopted her stylistic use of layering tracks, and Annie Lennox specifically incorporates Kate's style of exaggerated vocals into her repertoire. When Kate appeared on the scene in 1978, female vocalists were either from the Olivia Newton John school of innocence, or flaunted the flagrant sexuality of Debbie Harry. Kate, in contrast, was a mystery. She arrived on the scene pretty and blushing, claiming at every turn that she was an artist, *not* a body. There is no-one who could classify her in the naïve, good-girl mould after songs like 'Feel It', or complex imagery such as that in *The Dreaming*. Kate had, in a sense, opened the doors for female musicians, proving point in case that originality and intellect were acceptable, as was complex and unusual instrumentation. Dismissing allegations that her sexuality sold her albums, Kate went on to prove that she was very much a fore-running artist of the 80s, uninspired and uninfluenced by chart and review expectations. Kate Bush was the first woman to have a number 1 album in the history of UK music, pressing her point that gender was unimportant to the quality of music.

Certainly Kate was a pioneer of video as an art – specifically in 'Cloudbusting', and to a certain degree in 'Experiment Four', where she allows the storyline to take precedence over the music, and her lyrics to carry the song from strength to strength. She dismissed the idea that videos need be solely promotional, rather using them as a vehicle for making her music that much more complete. In the same manner that she used dance and other forms of movement to complement her singing, she intended her acting to complement her lyrics. Muchmusic, the 24-hour all-music cable channel in Canada, referred to Kate's work as a 'phenomenal contribution to the video field, opening doors for artists who felt a live performance was the extent of their abilities to get their music across.'

Justifiably, most critics draw a blank when trying to establish just who influenced Kate. With her imaginative and very often intellectual lyrics, Kate has managed to find inspiration in every walk of life, from books to films to nature. With subjects that could be considered either puerile or of 'issue' status, she has managed to create poignant and highly intelligible portraits of society and human beings. Her vocals are extraordinary, reminiscent of Susan Sarandon, if anyone, in the soundtrack to the *Rocky Horror Picture Show*. However, her voice has remained an enigma, both in her exploitation of it and in its amazing range and timbre. Even if one cannot comprehend the subject matter, the theatrics of her vocals allow a certain insight into her music which precludes the need for lyrical analysis.

Kate has attributed much of her vocal influence to her early appreciation of Lotte Lenya; however, her strength remains in her imagination and her uncanny grasp of recording technique and obscure instrumentation. The influences of folk music and classical instrumentals are undeniable; never have they been used to such a vibrant and comprehensive extent. Her total involvement in her music has allowed her to call upon the vast collection of stimuli she has hoarded over the years. On the occasions that she has complained of 'writer's block' she has only returned with yet more compelling and precocious music.

Kate Bush is truly an astounding musician, directing her life towards the perfection of her goals, focussing fully on her potential and the ultimate exploitation of it. She works in a rarified microcosm, enclosed in the protective bubble that the people she trusts have created for her. With love and support and at times creative input, her family and her boyfriend Del have nurtured her into the success story she has become. She trusts these people implicitly, not only for their warmth and security, but for the knowledge they have of her and her aspirations. It is to these people that she turns upon completion of a track. She notes: 'There's a small group that is around me that hears my new tracks. I can tell immediately from their reaction if it's any good or not . . . if it's not, well . . . then it's just shelved. I do need to be alone sometimes to gather myself together, but I need to have people around too. Anyone who writes needs contact with people to find out how they respond. I can't really see myself living in a commune.'

It is the people surrounding Kate who have provided the comfort and the freedom she needed to become what she is today. She acknowledges that she would be devastated if her family and close-knit group of friends were not there. They have capably managed her career financially and administratively, demanding the very best for Kate and the image she wishes to project. The confidence this inspires in Kate gives her the freedom to experiment in the comfortable knowledge that she is being well taken care of.

Kate's future is prepared for. With a studio of her own, numerous bestselling albums to her credit, and the directorship of no less than five of her own companies in her back pocket, Kate seems set for life Relinquishing none of her privacy or her home life for the sake of the success of her albums, she has balanced her life admirably. Even her record company appears entirely pleased with the state of her affairs, elusive as she may be. It is praiseworthy that someone with such a natural creativity and talent was not tempted by the trappings and the glamour of stardom when signed at such an early age. Kate Bush has made her own decisions from the beginning of her career, qualifying herself and her music in the eyes of the popular music world as something more than a capricious commodity. Holding fast to her beliefs, and for that matter her purse strings, Kate remains an extraordinary success story. 'Everyone has helped me so much and worked so hard – I've been really lucky on the whole.' Luck may have came into it, but primarily her success is born of talent and good sense. She has always been down to earth and methodical. And in her own words, '*Like it or not we were built tough . . . Like it or not we keep bouncing back/Because we're woman.*'

9
ANTICLIMAX

So much crying
I no longer see a future
. . . They took the game right out of it
'In Search Of Peter Pan'
Kate Bush, 1978

Following the release of *Never For Ever* on 8th September 1980, Kate was immediately encumbered with the typical EMI-style promotion, making personal appearances in Edinburgh, Glasgow, Liverpool, Manchester, Newcastle, Birmingham and London. Although she had begun putting together ideas for *The Dreaming* in early August, it was not until October that she was able to get anything down in demo form and get on with the actual writing process.

The Dreaming was to be an entirely Kate Bush-produced album, incorporating the technique she had picked up over the years. And with only herself at the helm, she had a chance to experiement more widely. As an amateur at producing, Kate was under a great deal of pressure to perform, to provide a showcase for her talents that would surpass anything she had done before, and being her own producer, there was no excuse for anything but exactly what she wanted. She said, 'It was a lot of responsibility to take on. And being a producer for the first time, I had to be aware of how much I was spending.' Not that Kate was generally aware of the financial arrangements that surrounded her success: a very patient EMI had footed the bill for her previous albums and with her brother taking care of the finances, she now immersed herself completely in the role of creating and performing. She affirms: 'I'm not a business woman at all. I just want to write and play and sing and dance. I don't feel I'm biting off too much. I understand my music better than others. I can judge. They can't'.

On 4th October, Kate established that she was deserving of the special treatment. Astonishingly for the third year in a row she was voted Best Female Singer in the *Melody Maker* poll. It would seem she had the midas touch. The promotion for *Never For Ever* continued into early November as she travelled to Germany and the Netherlands, appearing in live TV presentations across Europe. In late November Kate took the time to remix 'December Will Be Magic Again', this time persuading EMI to release it as a single in time for Christmas. It was released on 17th November and for the first time a single of Kate's appeared without a promotional video. Because of their hesitancy in supporting the track, there was no promotional budget allotted, and this may be why it received very little attention. The song reached only number 29 in the charts, after which it fizzled. It was incredibly successful in Israel, however, and in February of 1981 charted in the top ten.

Taking time off from the recording of *The Dreaming*, Kate teamed up with Peter Gabriel again to record a cover version of Roy Harper's song 'Another Day'. It was the same song that they had sung so successfully together on the forty-five minute TV special, 'Kate', the previous year, and they decided to release the track as a single. They attempted to co-write a B-side track and after several weeks came up with a song they titled 'Ibizza'. Because valuable time that she had intended to spend on her new album was passing quickly, and because the B-side met up to neither of their expectations, the project was shelved indefinitely. Just prior to this, Kate had recorded 'Warm and Soothing', which was also never released.

As her capabilities as a musician multiplied, she was becoming far less satisfied with her work, demanding inordinate feats from herself. At this time she actually stated that she 'hated' the sound of her voice on her first two albums. Feeling the limits of her previous songs, she was ready to develop new rhythms, incorporating and experimenting with various unusual instrumentals.

When 'Babooshka' became the number 1 hit from *Never For Ever* in December 1980, occupying the top ten spot around the world, the pressure to live up to expectations increased dramatically. Fan clubs were sprouting up across Canada, Australia and Europe and Kate was becoming a figure of international prestige. The USA again failed to succumb to her talents or her charms, although the underground music industry was developing a small cult following for Kate, and she was beginning to get some airplay on some of the smaller college networks.

She appeared in two special BBC Radio 1 music programmes where she played her music and chatted with host Paul Gambicini. There wasn't anywhere in the UK you could go to without encountering some aspect of the Kate Bush promotional carousel. To top it all, she was voted Best Female Artist for the third year running in the Capital Radio listeners' Poll. She commented after the awards ceremony: 'Success has changed me, but I think for the better. I've grown up a lot. It's really good that I am finally starting to sort out who I am and where I am going.'

It was back to the drawing board for Kate. She took two month's leave to sort out her ideas for the next album and prepare a structure within which she would produce it. Again she began demoing at the studio attached to her parent's farmhouse in Kent. She discusses the process: 'Well, most of the songs have a basic structure that are put either through a Fairlight or a drum machine, and then it's a kind of layering process. Then you get to a point, and it's normally quite early on with each song, where it starts to develop its own personality, and it's then really just doing what the song says, though there would obviously be sounds that would be wrong to go in a sad song, for instance. So it's just trying to choose the right textures.'

It is obvious that the Gabriel influence was increasing, as her creative process was now including the district use of the Fairlight. The first song written for *The Dreaming* was 'Sat In Your Lap' and Kate attributes her inspiration for that song to Stevie Wonder, whom she saw perform in September 1980. Describing her meeting with him after the concert, she gushed: 'I was thrilled to meet Stevie Wonder after his Wembley concerts, because he emanates a really beautiful vibe.'

She was a musician the whole world was getting to know. Her music often remained an enigma to even the most steadfast fans, but she was individual enough for a certain number of people to find her exceedingly distasteful. In April she was awarded both Most Liked and Least Liked Female Singer in a *Sunday Telegraph* opinion poll. Such were the conflicting impressions of her fame.

Recording for *The Dreaming* began in Townhouse Studio in May 1981 with Hugh Padgham engineering. Over the eight-week stint at Townhouse three tracks were recorded when Nick Launay took over the controls from Padgham. The absence of Jon Kelly was attributed to the fact that he had other commitments. Stuart Elliot, the drummer on *The Dreaming*, confirms: 'I don't think there was an absence of Jon Kelly or Andrew Powell for any particular reason. I mean, Jon Kelly would have been doing other projects for a start, so I mean they certainly didn't fall out either musically or personally. Jon Kelly does in fact rate a "special thanks" on the album sleeve – in all likelihood, it was due to the fact that he really did teach her all she knew.'

She had always been very concerned about the direction that her music would take, and it was only a natural progression to take over the production of it herself. Elliot goes on: 'I think she'd sat back and observed the mechanics behind production, and like most people in her position or my position, being in the studio, as you watch it you tend to think "Well, I could do that". She's always had very definite ideas about how she wants her music to be performed and produced, and every aspect of the thing has to be looked at in fine detail. It's hard for a producer or any one person to be involved in that all the time and keep their energy going, so I think people fell by the way on that album, a lot of people, a lot of engineers.'

The conflicts that were beginning to sprout during her work with Powell were evident as she demanded that all the musicians engineers and crew alike met her very high standards and ideals. 'I think it was really necessary that she had to do it herself', says Elliot, 'otherwise people would have left the room screaming'. The frustration of meeting her singular goal was not only time-consuming, but patience-trying. Elliot felt she was the only one with the patience to involve herself to the degree that she did.

The Dreaming was to be all Kate Bush, all her ideas, both in sound and lyric, as well as the finely engineered details that are the one creativity·an external engineer is allowed. Elliot found her easy to work with because he liked her, but he also didn't have any aspirations to put his 'stamp' on the album. 'Personally speaking,

I'll go to the end of the earth to find the right rhythm or drum sound that she wants and it doesn't bother me at all. But some people are so urgent and they want to put their own stamp on it and as a result of that they're not likely to last that long, which is why there probably are quite a few, engineers in particular, that worked on the album.'

Instead of following her usual practice of playing from demo right to the final track with all musicians present, playing 'live' as it were, Kate took a more 'one-to-one' tack, playing with or directing one musician at a time. Elliot for one found this technique disconcerting. 'At the time we were just doing drum tracks, whereas on the first albums we would be doing backing tracks with guitar, keyboards and everything, and the track would come to fruition at the end of the day. I always find that way of working odd. It's not the easiest way to work because it is not as spontaneous. It's exciting to influence the song that you are playing on, whereas when you're doing it on a one-to-one basis you can't influence what's already on tape. You can complement it, but you can't influence it.'

He found it difficult with Kate on the other side of the glass listening to every detail and therefore insisting it all be perfect. When she had embroiled herself in her piano playing in the past, these details had slipped by, and probably gave her earlier albums their less refined feel. She was one of the first musicians to use this technique – the layering of drum machines, keyboards, vocals and then drums – and it is a tradition that has developed since throughout the music industry. She did admit later, however, that having everyone play together was the most magical way of working, that she might not perfect every nuance of the song, but there was an atmosphere that developed, one that couldn't be created to the same degree on a solo basis.

It was a slow process, one that would take upwards of two years to complete from her first vision of the album. Alan Murphy sensed that things would be different on *The Dreaming* the first time he entered Townhouse Studios. 'We moved to the Townhouse which had been the output of all the great sounds that were coming out at that time – you know, the Phil Collins stuff and those kind of drum sounds which Kate was definitely moving towards. I think she wanted to try to capture some of that stuff in her music. It felt very different to me then. It felt that she had slightly changed the form, maybe she wouldn't play the piano. In fact, by this time, she would often sit in the control room the whole time while the track would be recorded . . . you know, drums, bass and one or two other instruments, and by this time of course she would be using the Fairlight quite a lot. So the form was changing, the locations were changing and the players to a certain extent were changing. New blood was brought in to try to cope with the different form and obviously it resulted in a completely different record.'

If Kate was spending increasing amounts of time in the control room, her burden only doubled. The recording would run until about two o'clock in the morning after which she would take the tapes home and listen to the results of her work until dawn. 'I've never been so involved in any project before,' she said. 'I just felt I had to produce this record myself to make sure it was different enough from anything else I've done. I admit I was scared.'

'Sat In Your Lap' was released on 21st June 1981 to flabbergasted critics. Where was the squeaky-voiced Kate they all knew and loved? They played the record, commented, and ended up with the general concensus that it was 'courageous' and 'unique'; no-one dared analyse it. She describes the meaning of the song: 'It's really about the frustration of having to wait for things – the fact that you can't do what you want to do now, you have to work towards it and maybe, only maybe, you'll get what you're after' She shrieks and pummels her way through her 'new' beat, alternating with a voice lower and softer than anyone had yet heard from Kate Bush. The acoustics are startling, and the Fairlight is very much in evidence, although not used to the extent that it is in the other numbers on the album. Her flair for dramatics is exaggerated to an uncanny degree and the lyrics are a confusing mass of repetitions and contradictions: '*Some say that heaven is hell some say that hell is heaven/. . . My cup she never overfloweth and 'tis I that moan and groaneth*'. Bad literature, astounding lyrics. The beat is unusual, she shifts unexpectedly from 3/4 to 4/4 and back, without altering vocal intensity. In July, Kate moved to Abbey Road, where she took on yet another engineer in the form of Haydn Bendall. It was here that she created the video for 'Sat In Your Lap'.

For seven weeks they worked on the backing tracks, breaking only once to fly to Dublin where Kate enlisted Planxty and the Chieftains

Kate, in the early days in front of her family fireplace. (*The Evening Standard, London*)

At the London Heathrow Airport in 1978. Fear of flying or just the noise? (*The Evening Standard, London*)

'We Anchor In Hope', Kate's local pub in her teens. (*Stage Broadcast, London*)

Kate with Cliff Richard, Labi Siffre and the London Symphony Orchestra prior to their guest appearances at London's Albert Hall celebrating the 75th Anniversary, 1979. (*Keystone Collection, London*)

Kate Bush and Bob Geldof,
winners of the *Melody Maker*
Reader's Poll Awards, 1979.
(*Keystone Collection, London*)

The Tour, 1979. Kate Bush
with illusionist Simon Drake.
(*Scope Features, London*)

Richard Aimes, tour manager for Kate Bush's critically acclaimed Tour of Life. (*Stage Broadcast, London*)

Stuart Elliot, session musician and drummer on a number of Kate's albums. Stuart Elliot remains a personal friend of Kate's. (*Stage Broadcast, London*)

'WOW', 1981. (Opposite) (*Joe Bangay, Buckinghamshire*)

Kate Bush and Anthony van Laast in a
scene from 'Wedding List' featured in her
own special show 'Kate' on London's
BBC2. (*Express Newspapers, London*)

Kate live on stage performing 'James and
the Cold Gun'. (*London Features International,
London*)

'Egypt', 1979 from
'Kate'. (*Rex Features,
London*)

Kate in Lord Lichfield's
book *The Most Beautiful
Women.* (*Patrick Lichfield,
Camera Press, London*)

Kate and Phil Collins at the BPI Awards 1987 where Kate won Best Female Vocalist. (*Express Newspapers, London*)

Kate and Del Palmer, celebrating the release of *Hounds of Love*, 1985. (*Alan Grisbrook, Camera Press, London*)

to back her on 'Night Of The Swallow'. She introduced a variety of old Irish instruments into the track – fiddle, uillean pipes, penny whistle and bouzouki – played and arranged to a certain degree by Bill Whelan, Liam O'Flynn, Sean Keane and Donnal Lunny. The song is highly illustrative of her increasing professionalism, and the success she was having in directing her talents to producing. It is a graceful, beautiful number, twisting and changing with every line. Her skill as a producer is evident in its orchestration, and instrumental complexity. She has reached supremacy in the control of her vocals, wafting in and out of the changing moods with extraordinary ease. 'Night Of The Swallow' was not released as a single, in the light of its distinct lack of commercial attributes, it is probably just as well.

The track established Kate as a serious musican and proved to be one of the pivotal works in her career. Where the 'serious' music critics had ignored her theatrics in the past, they stopped to take notice, and for the first time Kate was getting serious critical attention outside the pop circle.

It was time to move on again. In August, Kate moved to Oddessey Studios with Paul Hardiman assisting as engineer. It was finally a union that she felt comfortable with, as she worked with him from then through to the final remix.

A string of personal appearances filled the moments when she was out of the studio and she was featured on 'Razzmatazz', a children's show on which she explained the process behind the making of the video for 'Sat In Your Lap'; 'Looking Good Feeling Fit', a BBC TV programme where she described her dance regimen and her vegetarianism; 'Friday Night Saturday Morning', a talk show with Dr Desmond Morris describing her performances. She was one of the hostesses at a party held by EMI to celebrate fifty years of the operation at Abbey Road and was honoured by being asked to cut the cake with Helen Shapiro. Finally, after an exhausting interview lasting several days for a US production, 'Profiles In Rock', Kate took a well-deserved break, returning to the studio in late January to prepare the final dubs. Aside from a trip to Loch Ness, Kate used the main part of her holiday to rework some of the tracks, adding and removing lyrics and backing vocals.

Her return from Loch Ness saw yet another studio change, and she moved, with Paul Hardiman, to Advision Studios where she remained for the final five months before the album was ready for release. In April she was ready. But yet again EMI were not, and for numerous promotional reasons they postponed the launch of her album until September. Freed from the hectic publicity that would have ensued had the album been released on schedule, Kate left for Jamaica for several weeks, coming back to work with Zaine Griff on her tribute to Kemp's *Flowers*.

Zaine Griff was a cohort from the days of Lindsay Kemp's classes and she called upon Kate to sing backing vocals for the obvious reason that, 'Kate was the only person I knew who would understand the link between music and movement.' The single was released in July, and disappeared into oblivion immediately. In late July, Kate was asked, with only forty-eight hours notice, to fill in for David Bowie who was unable to attend the first Prince's Trust Rock Gala at the Dominion Theatre in London. With little time to rehearse, she chose 'The Wedding List', one of the most vibrant tracks from *Never For Ever*. Backed by Phil Collins on drums, Gary Brooker on keyboards, Pete Townsend and Midge Ure on guitars and Mick Karn on bass, she was greeted with resounding applause, capturing headlines the following days in the majority of the London papers. The highlight of the evening was when Kate's dress gave up its attempt to contain her curves, and broke a spaghetti string which she artfully caught and held for the remainder of the performance. Flushed and giggling, Kate was nonetheless the star of the evening; 'Kate Bush (what ever happened to?) danced onstage for one number impressing the crowds, . . . but leaving some of us wondering what that song was. . . .' noted Carol Clerk of *Melody Maker*, while Sunie of the *Record Mirror* claimed, 'Best moment by far was Kate Bush's number, a storming success . . .'. Despite the fact that she was limited by a hand mike and the weak accoustics of the Dominion Theatre, Kate capably stole the evening. After the performance, Pete Townsend was quoted as saying, 'Her predicament just went to show the power of prayer . . . all the roadies backstage were praying for a glimpse of Kate's body . . . and they nearly got their wish.' Prince Charles quipped, 'I must confess . . . that I always think BPI stands for the British Pornographic Industry.'

The title track of *The Dreaming* was released on 27th July 1982, achieving excellent reviews and a great deal of approval though qualified, from the music Press. The radio stations weren't so kind, however, and because EMI had blanched at the lack of commercial value in the album and the lack of an obvious single choice, the record received little airplay. Aside from David 'Kid' Jensen, who played a Kate 'Three-of-the-best' on BBC Radio 1, the track was not played at all at the station. There was considerable disappointment when on 'Roundtable', a Radio 1 review show featuring guest musicians, the panel attacked the album, claiming it was Kate's worst record since 'Wuthering Heights', and wondering whether one could really call it 'Rock Music'. There were no information sheets or Press releases from EMI to accompany the record, only a handwritten, last-ditch attempt of Kate's to explain the track. She wrote:

The Dreaming

The Aboriginals are not alone in being pushed out of their land by modern man, by their diseases, or for their own strange reasons. It is very sad to think they might all die. 'The Dreaming' is the time for Aboriginals when humans took the form of animals, when spirits were free to roam and in this song as the civilized begin to dominate, the 'original ones' dream of the dreamtime.

Again a song with 'issue status', it was looked upon with scepticism, the same reaction she had initially encountered with 'Breathing'. Tim De Lisle of *Smash Hits* wrote: 'The oddball single to end all oddball singles . . . very bizzare . . . strictly for Aborigines . . .' The reception was generally disappointing, the single being misunderstood on most fronts, and classed, with Kate, as unmistakeably weird. Because it was her most serious work to date, a strong subject and incredibly complex in its use of percussion and instrumentation, it could have been seen as chance to establish herself once and for all as a serious and capable musician. But the critics remained baffled. Kate reacted by stating: 'It was disappointing. My song doesn't seem to fit in with what's happening at the moment. I just can't relate to the singles chart.' She also noted that she was much more of an albums artist, a term that didn't yet qualify in 80s rock. A song about the complex plight of the Aborigines in the face of the cruel, usurping mineral prospectors, Kate claimed that her inspiration for the song was 'this book which is all about Aborigines and Australian art and it's called *The Dreaming*. The song wa originally called "Dreamtime", but when I found out that the other word for it was "The Dreaming", it was so beautiful – just by putting the "The" in front of "Dreaming" made something very different and so I used that.'

The title, *The Dreaming*, suggests something quiet and dreamlike, so the shock of the chanting, animalistic soundtrack is disconcerting. The production of the track began with the drum pattern on a Linn Drum machine. Piano and three tracks of guiding vocals were added and then synthesized with her trusty Fairlight. Then came Rolf Harris on the didgeridoo, smashing marble and plates, African drums miked inside to create extra emphasis, and Percy Edwards recreating the animal noises of the Australian outback. The track displays a highly sophisticated use of external sound, put through numerous stages of harmonizers to create a haunting, melodramatic and fascinating track. She described it as her most complex album to date, justifying the near-two years since anyone had heard anything from her.

In an attempt to make up for EMI's lack of promotional interest, Kate took matters into her own hands, appearing live at a special Radio 1 Roadshow in the piazza at London's Covent Garden and making a personal appearance at the Virgin Megastore at Oxford Street in London. The video for the single wasn't shown until late August, well past peak promotion time. Despite EMI's lackadasical attitude to the track it remained unaffected by the reviews and entered the charts. It peaked at only number 48, and its stay was limited to an embarrassing three weeks. The album itself was released on 13th September, surprising its critics by entering the charts at number 3. The album eventually went gold.

The Dreaming is the most difficult of Kate's albums to listen to. The overuse of percussion and synthesizer becomes repetitive to the point of annoyance. She put a label on the sleeve requesting that the album be played loud, but the result of obeying her wish is a throbbing headache. It is an ambitious, even overproduced, album full of unconventional tracks and untypical Bush vocals. Her voice is used once again as a warped instrument, but the ferocity of feeling keeps it more even and controlled. The lyrics range from utterly confusing to obsessively melodramatic, focusing on the Aboriginal plight in 'The Dreaming', and jumping over to the horrifying Vietcong for 'Pull Out The Pin'.

'Pull Out The Pin' is a frightening and poignant account of a Vietcong guerilla preparing to kill his white victim as he clutches his silver buddha in his mouth. Dave Gilmour is obviously apparent in the background vocals and the sound of helicopters and guitars has been synthesized to create an echoing percussion. Even-timbred, Kate's voice only rises to her raunchiest, rockest Carole Pope-like best in the lines '*I love life . . .*'. The impact is phenomenal. The fear, the gutteral sounds and the sweating anticipation are all captured in the song and it could well be considered her most successful 'drama' yet.

'There Goes A Tenner', which was the next single to be released from *The Dreaming*, is another mini-drama, describing the attempt of pretty crooks to blow a safe. Acquiring an extraordinary cockney-type accent, she narrates the saga in a stylish alto. The doubts of the thieves which beset them the evening before their job are interestingly reflected in the alterations of the vocals, and the characters come alive in the strong images she produces. Taking on the characteristics of Cagney and Raft she produces a 30s-style number, jazzy and lighthearted despite its centrally dangerous theme. She notes, '. . . so it's like maybe they get a bit cocky . . . I dunno. I think that in a situation like that you'd almost try to be like the person you admire so perhaps they'd be like Cagney and George Raft. That idea was nothing really deep – it was just handy . .. for me, Cagney is one of the greatest actors that has ever been.' Again, her curious imagination came up with a vivid, lurid play on the old movies, her exaggerated accents making it a parody.

She claims 'Get Out Of My House' and 'Leave It Open' are attempts to analyse very complex personal emotions, but they are harsh and unmusical numbers, replete with slamming doors and bawdy, hoarse hollering. The last line of 'Leave It Open' perhaps describes best Kate's final succumbing to her imagination: '*Say what we're gonna let in/We let the weirdness in*'. The songs defy any analysis; one just has to take Kate's word for their meaning. She said about 'Get Out Of My House', 'The idea with the song is that the house is actually a human being who's been hurt and he's just locking all the doors and not letting anyone in. The person is so determined not to let anyone in that one of his personalities is a concierge who sits in the mouth, stands at the door and says, "You're not coming in here!".' Similarly, 'Leave It Open' 'is the idea of human beings being like cups – like receptive vessels. We open and shut ourselves at different times . . . you should be able to control your levels of receptivity to a productive end'.

Perhaps the most typical Kate Bush numbers on the album are 'All The Love' and 'Houdini' where she uses her voice at its haunting best. 'Houdini' is based on the age-old story of Houdini's death and his widow Bess's faith that their love was immortal and that he would be contacting her from the other side. It is one of the most flattering songs for Kate's voice and has the feel of a rich, colourful old ballad. She felt very emotional about the song: 'I thought it was both a very romantic and a very sad image because, by passing that key, she is keeping him alive – she's actually giving him the key back to life.' The key became a central image in the promotion of the album. Numerous posters were printed featuring the line 'With a Kiss I'd Pass the Key' with Kate looking particularly sultry.

'All the Love' deals with the feelings of guilt, remorse, and regret that accompany the love not only of one's partner, but of friends and colleagues. Sung in a lower register than usual, Kate mournfully assesses things that might have been. Whispers, sighs, soft breathing dovetail in and out of the melody creating a tiny symphony of soft sound. Her ability to project herself into the role is astonishing, the strength of her voice varying with each emotion. It is one of the factors that makes the album a challenging and unusual listen despite its lack of commercial bite.

'Suspended In Gaffa' has the same ethnic flavour as 'Kashka From Baghdad' on *Lionheart*, and in all territories but the UK it was released as a single in the place of 'There Goes A Tenner'. 'There Goes A Tenner' was referred to as the 'lost single' and went virtually unnoticed and generally unplayed, but 'Suspended In Gaffa' made it into the top ten in charts around the world, excluding, of course, the US which remained an impossible nut to crack. 'Gaffa' is a livelier track than most on the album, and more accessible. In an interview with Paul Simper of *Melody Maker*, Kate explained the song: 'Lyrically it's not really that dissimilar to "Sat In Your Lap" in saying that you really want to work for some things [talking about

God and purgatory] so it was almost like you had to sit here until he decided to come back . . . you see the potential for perhaps getting somewhere very special and that excites me a lot and it's the idea of working towards that end perhaps one day, when you're ready for that change. It's like entering a different level of existence, where everything goes slow-mo . . . it's almost a religious experience.'

Lines like, '*But sometimes its hard/To know if I'm doing it right/Can I have it all?*' perhaps aptly describe what Kate was feeling in the production of *The Dreaming*, she was ready to move on to different levels and different aspects of her music, but was held back by public and corporate expectation, and of course the limits of her own capabilities, which were still in the process of development. *The Dreaming* is an album that reflects her in-between stage, something between the more infantile and commercial *Never For Ever*, and the extravagant mastery of *Hounds Of Love*. She was just beginning to grasp hold of the tools that the studio and various instruments had to offer, and *The Dreaming* displays an overabundance of stimuli; it is an overproduced album with far too many external effects marring the clean lines that shaped *Never For Ever*.

The Dreaming only lasted one week at number 3, falling to number 7 the next and out entirely after only four weeks. It was a disappointment to many fans, who had been waiting for over two years for its release. There were others, though, who were much more appreciative of the album, calling it a 'turning point in rock history', the beginning of progressive, or 'Art' rock, a term that would be used more and more frequently as the decade went on. It is an album that shunned all convention, ignoring the dictates that there should be songs within it for single release, and it confused EMI to the extent that they were unable to come up with any sort of comprehensive and effective promotional plan. The songs *need* explanation. The difference between *The Dreaming* and her previous album was so marked that people were already beginning to speculate about the next album.

Kate was obviously nonplussed about the relative failure of the album, but because it continued to sell, eventually going gold, she kept her favour with EMI. The opinion that Kate was ten years ahead of her time continued to hold true. She felt frustrated with the pressure to come up with singles: 'Maybe its wrong to see me as a pop personality. You're going to keep changing – "Wuthering Heights" was a story with music and dancing, but I've changed so much since then. The things that the media most remember about me are those things. Some people see that I am changing but . . . oh, not as many as the people who hang onto those singles.'

The Dreaming is of an autobiographical nature, recording struggles and love and relationships and all the things that tangle day-to-day life. If there is a tangible theme, it must be progression, living, carrying on. And that is what she fully intended to do.

10
CATHARSIS

Well I'm not sure if I want to be up here at all
And I'd like to be back on the ground
But I don't know how to get down

'Kite'
Kate Bush, 1978

The promotional machine was set to work after *The Dreaming* failed to make any impact beyond it's meagre number 3 position in the charts, and a disillusioned, quieter Kate put up with endless criticism, hours and hours of explanation of the album and rampant rumours that she had 'fizzled'. In September 1982 she travelled to Europe, stopping in Munich to perform 'The Dreaming' single and received a gold disc for sales of *Never For Ever* in Germany. There were constant pressures to justify the new album, and to explain why she had changed so drastically what had been a winning formula. Heedless of the generally poor publicity, Kate continued to Milan and then back to the UK where she appeared on a number of BBC TV programmes, and made personal appearances in the northern parts of the country. In Birmingham she was interviewed by Paul Gambaccini for the BBC programme 'Pebble Mill At One', where she discussed the new album and her plans for the future. Portions of the video for 'There Goes A Tenner' were featured and, as had been the fate of the single, the video received its one and only airing.

Moving on to France, Kate spent a lot of time promoting 'Suspended In Gaffa', the international single which wasn't released in the UK. The response to the single was a dramatic improvement over that for 'There Goes a Tenner', and uneasy EMI executives were chastized for an unsuitable UK single choice. Back in

Germany, she was greeted with an immense fanfare, with 'Gaffa' well placed in their top ten chart. Her Australian and Canadian following was growing and there were constant demands for her to tour, or at least to involve herself in some personal publicity. *The Dreaming* was making an impact for the first time in the US, entering the Billboard Top 200. It was the first of Kate's albums to do so, and EMI, excited by the change in attitude, spent the next few years flooding the market with Kate Bush albums, videos and promotional paraphernalia. By the end of the year *The Dreaming* was listed in the top ten of US Progressive radio stations for the previous year. With an album that had failed so miserably in her homeland she had broken the silence and entered what had become her biggest challenge – the US market.

She was exhausted. Some say her spirit was entirely broken. Plans for a tour and for an autobiographical account, provisionally entitled *Leaving My Tracks*, were shelved indefinitely. Kate Bush disappeared.

The pressures of an unsuccessful album by previous standards, the constant misinterpretation of her music and the strain of promoting an album that no-one but she was behind had been too much for Kate. She toyed with the idea of leaving the record industry, having found that her initial ambition just to write and sing – get just ten songs on a piece of plastic – had become a stressful and pretentious carousel. Her private life had been invaded and she had, for the last five years, lost all contact with herself, the Kate inside the superstar.

The first thing on her agenda was to leave London. The frantic pace of the city was wearing her down in what little free time that she had, and she took the opportunity to move with Del to a tiny cottage in Kent, a mere thirty minutes from her parents' home. She was able to find the peace for which she had been searching so long: 'We moved to the country and that helped me relax. I am not the kind of person who enjoys living in London and I needed to get away and spend time on my life because until then I had never stopped. I'd been in the business continually from a young age and never had a proper break.'

She took the time to re-evaluate her life, to make sure that the direction she was taking was the one she really wanted to be following. *The Dreaming* had marked an escape from her previous style, and had been met with little acclaim. The way she wanted to progress with her music seemed unluctrative and displeased her record company. From that point of view there was a choice: either create music to please herself, or forego her integrity and produce what the public wanted to hear. It was difficult. 'I wasn't sure what I wanted then, and became frightened of the exposure . . . Being so vulnerable I didn't know if I just wanted to be famous or just make a record I was happy with.' It was a quieter, more reflective Kate Bush who left the music scene in 1982; the vivacious, sparkling darling of pop with her constant stream of 'Wows' and 'Incredibles' had vanished inside the seemingly much older, rather wan woman she had become.

The enormous quantity of chocolate and unhealthy food she had become accustomed to during the hectic period following *The Dreaming* had left her pale and unhealthy, and it was obvious that there was something very wrong. She remembers, 'I was just a complete wreck, physically and mentally. I'd wake up in the morning and find I couldn't move . . . eventually I went to see my Pa.' She remembers her father was extremely worried about her condition, which was diagnosed as nervous fatigue and stress generally: she was totally run down. It was time to analyse her position and allow herself to live a more normal life, something she hadn't been able to do for over five years.

EMI were not pleased that Kate picked this time to disappear from the scene. The periods between albums were becoming longer and longer and after the phenomenal cost of producing and recording *The Dreaming*, which failed to reimburse them to the degree they had expected, they were hot on Kate's tail for a new album. For the first time she shunned them completely. It was well known that EMI had invested a great deal more money in their little protégée than they had in anyone else in the stable, and they were becoming impatient with her absolute refusal to comply with their wishes. Bemused by *The Dreaming*, they had neglected to support her in the manner to which she had been accustomed, and which she deserved. It was perhaps the thought there just might not be anything else to come from Kate Bush that led EMI to make such great efforts to exploit her previous albums in the newly acquired market in the US.

In June 1983 EMI America released a mini-album containing five tracks to feed the embryonic market that was beginning to show signs of interest. Provoking Kate no end, they finally persuaded her to do a promotional tour of the States, even though they were aware of her fatigue and her need for a break. After *The Dreaming* it must have been difficult for Kate to face having to explain the early music from which she had progressed to such a degree. She found her first two albums 'childish' and complained of the amateur quality of her voice. The tour was cancelled when the *QE2* was put out of service because of technical difficulties. Refusing, as she had in the past, to fly, the promotion was shelved and EMI had to comfort themselves by preparing reams of publicity with which they quickly infiltrated the stations.

In July 1983 the US mini-album stormed into the Billboard Top 200, and EMI made arrangements for the *Live At Hammersmith* video to be circulated. The feeling was that with the new, genuine interest in her music, the market couldn't help but be seduced further by her most impressive stage presence. EMI carried the extensive promotion well into the following year, supplying an enormous back-catalogue of Kate Bush material, re-releasing *Lionheart* and *Never For Ever*, and under a stunning new banner, 'Looking Back To See Ahead' made a concerted effort to relaunch Kate Bush in the US as the greatest female pop star yet to come out of the UK. Rumours of her going over to promote fuelled the attention she was getting, and almost immediately *Lionheart* responded by entering the top 200. She'd done it. From a small underground cult following of fans, she had progressed into the realms of American music history. The pressure increased. With her new audience now also demanding a new album, and countries around the world requesting her presence at all sorts of local events, Kate was thrown yet again into the turmoil of keeping up her image. She was firm this time about dates of delivery for the album, making it clear that they would get it when, and only when, she was finished. Fraught with the increasing expense of studio time and the pressures that incurred, she began to think seriously about building her own studio – a place where she could create at her own speed, and somewhere that she could call home. The question was where to build it.

'It's like our house. One day we suddenly stumbled across it and a back door had been left open so were were able to go inside. I'm sure there's a kind of force, a magnetic energy saying "Come in, we're meant for each other".' Kate's father took the time to hunt around for suitable properties on which to build the studio, but without success. She confirms: 'It had always been an ambition of mine to have my own studio, so once we found a house we set about putting one together in the back garden. Although I can work under a certain amount of pressure, paying £90 per hour at Abbey Road got to be too much. It also meant having to travel into London every day which can be pretty exhausting.' Having her own studio was in itself a relief to Kate. Having made the decision to proceed and work on another album despite the flop of the previous one, it now seemed a simpler process by which to proceed. She explains her thinking at the time: 'Obviously after the last album at the end of 1982 where I'd just spent an intense period in the studio doing it, I wanted to have a break. I felt that I hadn't really had any time to take things in because I'd been working so constantly, really since 1978, and we'd just moved out of London, so I just wanted to spend some time at home, see my friends, take in new stimuli, try and create a new energy for an album that would be different from the one I'd just written. And also I wanted to get together our own recording studio, which was definitely something that was being pointed at all the way through the other albums – it was *the* thing to do. I think during the time that I was taking off to discover things, write, get the studio together, I made some of the most important decisions, and very beneficial ones, that I have made. I think it's all good. I understand what you mean about that time – [being away from the Pop scene can create all kinds of difficulties in returning] – and in a way you get scared that you are spending so long away that you won't be able to come back. The priority, and again, I really did feel this, was what I wanted during this time: the work, not necessarily being successful or famous; that what I was working on could be the best it could be at that time.'

Her integrity had won over the commercial pressures, and enlivened by the decisions she was making, and the new move, she prepared to complete the studio. 'I was involved with the design. Really the inspiration behind the whole project was my father. He was totally encouraging and he really did put a lot of it together himself. He was in there building it and advising and putting the structure together, so really the studio is a lot to do wth his effort and enthusiasm.' The close-knit family continued to support her as she took time off, and she really got to know them again. Simply by releasing her from some of the hassle in the building of the studio, her father had yet again succeeded in comforting and taking care of his daughter. The business side of her life was being capably taken care of by her brother and Del, and the rest of her family pampered her emotionally while she got back on her feet again. 'I think they are supportive to me in every area possible. I think I am most definitely a strongly emotionally-based person, and my family are totally integral to everything I do because I love them.' She needed the support. Unwilling to divulge any of her private life to an already overbearing record company, she refused to allow any of her personal difficulties to enter into her relationship with them. The support of her family was essential. 'I think it is something that has always been there and if it wasn't there it would probably be devastating for me.'

During the time that she rested from her intense life in the limelight, she kept up a good if slightly cool relationship with EMI, firmly standing by her statement that the album would be finished only when she was ready. Remembering the pressure they had applied in the past, forcing her to finish albums she was just not ready to present, made her reaffirm her position with them. 'The priority is to make the thing [the record] as good as you can, and the situation with the record company is that I work on the album and when it's finished I present it to them. I think as long as they're happy with the album we have a very good relationship. I just have to hold the priorities in my head, really, and try to forget the pressures, but it can be very difficult because the longer it takes the more worried you get about sustaining the right energy and making it good. I think you just have to hang on in there and go for it.'

Despite the lack of success with *The Dreaming*, relations with EMI stayed fairly good. She felt that she couldn't give them an unfinished album, so it was a matter of waiting until the album was finished. 'It's not through choice that it takes so long. It's not something that you can force. You just have to work hard and when it's finished, it's finished.'

Aside from exhaustion being a reason for her decision to leave the scene for a few years, there was also the problem of 'writer's block' which she claimed to have contracted for the first time. 'It took me four or five months to be able to even write again. It's very difficult when you've been working for years, doing one album after another. You need fresh things to stimulate you.'

She found much stimulus in the new world that now surrounded her, full of green spaces and natural wildlife. Gone was the cement jungle and the maelstrom that success had pressured her with. 'I wanted to spend some time at home with my boyfriend and the cats. I just wanted to do the things that I'd forgotten about, like going to the cinema, and for walks and seeing people again. That's why I decided to take a bit of the summer out and . . . just relax. Not being Kate Bush the singer, just being myself.' She isolated herself for six months, reading, watching television, listening to classical music. She actually lost touch entirely with the popular music scene. 'It was an incredible period of isolation. When I restarted work on the album I found there were times when I didn't even know what was in the charts.' She reflected that the chart artists were not all that important to her. She felt that she was not truly a pop star in the sense that the production of commercial singles was not high on her list of priorities. She commented that she couldn't believe the rubbish that was making its way into the charts at that time.

She found freedom and happiness in her soujourn. 'It was wonderful when I took months and months off after my last album. I'd cook us a vegetarian meal each evening and we had time at home to grow vegetables and watch TV together and do all the sort of nice ordinary things that I hadn't had time to do since I started making records.' The new happiness she found with Del was reflected in her next album, *Hounds Of Love*, and she came out from hiding flushed and girlishly enthusiastic about her 'man'. The album's thematic basis was in the complexities of love, but far more honestly, and without the dramatics of her previous albums. It is a mature love that Kate Bush sings about, and there is no need to speculate about the period when she was out of sight: it was a maturing of bonds, a growth from the adolescent analysis of love to a treasuring and knowing approach to adult love. The change was phenomenal.

The studio gave her the freedom to work at her own speed. She could stop to relax in the comfort of her home, knowing that the cost in hours was not escalating. In September 1983, she was ready to venture into the studio and begin some elementary demoing, taking time to write at her own pace. She worked on the new album for the remainder of that year and the next one and a half. In November 1983, they released one of her favourites from *The Dreaming*, 'Night Of The Swallow', in Eire, where it was received with much enthusiasm. It was one of the first good initial reactions she received for any of the numbers on the album.

In order to fill in the gaps that Kate's disappearance had left in their line-up, EMI released the *Single File* box set, a collection of her eleven best singles to date, plus the 'On Stage' EP and a remix of 'Ne T'Enfuis Pas', the French language version of 'Don't Fly Away' which had been released in France and Canada backed with 'Un Baiser D'Enfant', the French 'Infant Kiss'. They were all produced with picture sleeves and an accompanying booklet. This was the only occasion on which her two French tracks were distributed in the UK; an attempt by Canifer, a leading record importer, to release them in 1983 ended in threat of court action by EMI and an immediate quashing of plans.

As the time between albums seemed to grow interminable, various rumours about Kate Bush began to fly about. Speculators insisted that she was preparing to leave EMI and that the construction of her own studio verified the fact that she would be working independently from then on. Hilary Walker refused to comment, and executives at EMI shrugged their shoulders, not making very much effort to squash any rumours. A blurred photo of Kate appeared in the *Daily Mail*, picturing her as having blown to an unlikely eighteen stone. The tabloids jumped at the chance to chastise Kate for overeating and various headlines screamed that the little sparrow of UK rock had blown up into an ungainly monster. Several weeks later, however, Kate was pictured at her normal seven or eight stone, her tiny frame as curvacious and attractive as it had ever been.

There were more rumours that Kate had a serious drug problem, that she was being treated in French or Caribbean rehabilitation centres, which explained her disappearance from the scene. There had been much speculation previously about Kate's drug taking. One artist who worked with her, who has asked to remain unnamed, stated that Kate did smoke drugs, and that her brothers, both post-generation hippies, had continued to smoke from their teenage years. Kate, having difficulty with the consumption of alcohol, apparently found this the most comfortable manner in which to relax and create. These rumours are just hearsay, things that float about the music industry, not an unusual state of affairs when a high profile musician is absent from the scene for an extended period. There doesn't appear to be any basis in fact. There are no records of her checking into a rehabilitation centre, nor are the people around her willing to confirm that she has ever, even if infrequently, been known to take drugs.

Kate was inspired by her new surroundings. In an unofficial meeting, she confessed to feeling certain that *Hounds Of Love* would be her best album yet. She had lost some of her fear of returning to the scene and later commented; 'I actually thought it would be much harder coming back than it was. I feel more excited about everything now than I was when I had my first hit seven years ago.'

The time had allowed her to refocus her ideals, to create an album that would satisfy both herself and EMI and inevitably the record-buying public. They needn't have worried. She had crossed what was to be the only valley in her career, and was ready to go. Back to the top, of course.

11
CLIMAX

All the colours look brighter now
Everything they say seems to sound new
Slipping into tomorrow too quick
'Oh To Be In Love'
Kate Bush, 1978

Business was booming in Kate's absence, with the Americans finally taking notice and the unexpected success of her *Single File* Box in both countries. The video, entitled simply *Single File*, that accompanied the box was a compilation of all the promotional videos from 'Wuthering Heights' to 'There Goes A Tenner'. Within two weeks of its release it became the bestselling music video in the UK. The realization that her career was soaring without her physical presence in the promotion, came as a relief to Kate and she felt less pressurized to finish the current album and rush back to the scene. In June 1984 Kate began overdubbing and preparing the final mixes and remixes for *Hounds Of Love*, allowing a full twelve months to perfect the songs to her approval.

In June 1985, it was ready. This fifth album had taken longer to complete than any of the preceding ones and Kate was becoming aware that she would have to allot herself progressively longer periods of time in which to create. 'In a way you do get scared that you are spending so long away that you won't be able to come back. The priority – and again, I really did feel this is what I wanted during this time – was the work and not necessarily being successful or famous; that what I was working on could be the best it could be at the time. I wanted to get away from the exposure, the being consumed that can start to happen to you if you don't get away. I think, too, when I spend so long on projects, I want to get back to it more and more when I'm out doing promotion because I know that everything takes me such a long time to do . . . I do find things take me longer than I thought they would. It's not something that I plan; the work takes over, and in order to make it better you just have to be patient and spend more time with it, obviously.'

Her attitude to *Hounds Of Love* was different to the previous ones. Having taken the steps to get her own studio together, she felt confident enough to improvise and to experiment with new sounds. The pressure of spending enormous amounts of money in the studio had been removed, and she allowed herself and her musicians more freedom in the production of the tracks. Her family was present a great deal of the time, and the whole atmosphere became more relaxed and, in turn, much more creative. Alan Murphy, who had worked on most of her previous albums, and on three tracks of the fifth album, comments: 'It was a fantastic feeling. We were very close to the family. Kate's mum and dad were around all the time, and that in itself is a great feeling when you're working in her studio. Of course Paddy's there all the time. There was a completely different feel by that stage – it was just like recording in someone's front room. If it had been possible for Kate to do that eight years ago she would have done so; but of course you have to learn all the options and the only way to learn them is to go out into the world and learn them and pick up the things you like and bring them back to your base . . . it's a very, very nice studio with all the latest electronics; the desk, the tape machines, a Fairlight III – it's really come on.'

Using her 'layering' technique, Kate worked from the original demo instead of preparing separate tapes. This process allowed her to keep the 'magical' sensation that she felt she had lost on *The Dreaming* by producing separate tracks for each instrument and *then* amalgamating them. The new process allowed her original ideas and concepts for the song to show through in each stage of the production, and the musicians could actually hear their own contribution to the sound. Alan Murphy expands: 'Now Kate has everything set up. If she comes up with an idea it goes straight onto tape, and that is the tape that everyone works on. At other times what happens is that you do a cassette demo first of all, and then you try to move that on to an eight-track demo so that you can get some ideas and fill up a few tracks and find out which way the song is going. And then you take it into the studio and say to the band, "This is the demo, what can we do with it?" Inevitably something goes missing. It's very difficult to put your finger on it. It's not what anybody does or doesn't play; it's just that something goes missing along the line. Lots of bands –the Eurythmics specifically – do this as well as making the demo, the master, and I think that's what Kate has learned to do. It's her craft now, and a very worthwhile one at that; never giving the musicians the opportunity to lose their work because it's always part of the basic canvas rather than having to transfer. There's never any of that involved. If the idea works on tape then it won't be lost. It's much more relaxed, and as a player . . . it just enables you to let your ideas out much easier, and at the end of the day you're just not pressurized.'

Kate came up with a number of tracks, many of which had to be shelved because they didn't fit in with the theme of the album. Because the second side of the album, separately entitled 'The Ninth Wave', was what Kate called a 'concept', in other words, a strong set of images with a working theme that are carried through the entire side, she had to delete several songs from the album because they just didn't have the same feeling. For the first time Kate actually rewrote songs, changing the emphasis or the rhythm to synchronize with the message or the over-riding tempo of the work. 'I normally find that I throw lots of ideas down, and then coming back to them in a few days time I would see that they weren't as good as they could be, so I would just literally leave them and not finish off the track. On the second side of the album I had one and a half tracks rewritten because the whole flow of the side needed to be changed, because the whole nature of it kept changing as things were being put on top of the basics.'

Kate said of *Hounds of Love*: 'For me, this album is like two quite separate pieces of work – the A-side is very much five individual songs that are in some way all linked by love as the theme, and this seemed to be a title that really did sum up that side. We actually gave a title to the B-side too, but because you can't have two titles for one album we just went for the A-side title to cover it all.'

'The Ninth Wave' was the most time-consuming side, as Kate fought to ensure that the songs led into one another, and that their relationship with one another was evident. She explains her ideology: 'It's about someone who comes off a ship, and they've been in the water all night by themselves, and it's about that person re-evaluating their life from a point which they've never seen before. It's about waking up from things and being reborn – going through something and coming out the other side very different'. If the initial concept seems rather simple, the lyrics preclude such criticism. This is truly Kate Bush at her best, moulding, creating, linking her tracks to create a continuous melody, with only slight variations from her theme. It sounds like an excellent soundtrack: her idea from the beginning was to produce the second side as a film. From different perspectives, Kate's narrators look at various aspects of nature, and it becomes evident that Kate's sojourn with nature was incredibly inspiring. 'A lot of the imagery for the whole piece came from moving out of London, in that I was surrounded much more by the elements than people and man-made things: the power of things like the wind in the trees. I mean, it sounds corny, but it's very earthy and I think it does affect you. And also, some war films covered people coming out of ships or planes into the sea in situations where they were alone and frightened. The sea is so enormous and so unknown and taken for granted I don't think people consider the cruel side of the sea – how ultimate it is – and also the whole thing of sensory deprivation when you've been in the water for a while and start losing all sense of where you are, who you are, whether you're upside down or whatever. I just found the whole thing terribly fascinating and, although a very physical event, also very much a mental event – that you were travelling in your head even though your body was just floating in water.'

There isn't the same strenuous attempt to be original on *Hounds Of Love* as there was on *The Dreaming*, and the power of her voice is used to its natural extreme, rather than exploited and misaligned through overuse of the synthesizer. Kate Bush does *not* screech in *Hounds Of Love*. This is a mature album, a thoughtful and professional exposé of her talents, which have developed to reflect accurately her ideas and her emotions without the dependence on electronic equipment and shrill, unnatural instrumentation. One of the features of the album is the obvious individuality of the musicians left, for the first time under Kate's direction, to their own resources. Stuart Elliot, who was responsible for the drums on the album, discusses her different technique: 'There was quite a break, I think it was maybe eighteen months or a couple of years later [after *The Dreaming*] that Kate sent me the demos for the *Hounds Of Love*. It was the usual piano/vocal thing, but this time she sent a letter with it explaining what each track was about and roughly how she felt it should go. It was the first time she'd ever done that – she'd never, ever dealt in demos at all apart from on the day when you're supposed to be performing the music. And that gave me a couple of weeks to think about what she wanted and what would spring into my mind and it was quite nice. After I'd received the letter I checked into her studio and we started working on the tracks. It was a lot easier working that way, having heard them a little bit before.'

Alan Murphy was given similar freedom on 'Waking The Witch', one of the most successful tracks on the 'Ninth Wave' side. An upbeat powerful number, it revolves around the torture of a witch who confesses her guilt in order to escape, at which time she is put at the mercy of the people who demand her death. The backing vocals put to shame any production of Macbeth's witches on stage, and Kate's girlish voice soars in and out in a witch-like chant. The song is a great success, beginning with voices from her past – teachers, parents, friends – trying to awaken her, and ending with the brisk sound of a chopper and the voice calling over a megaphone to 'Get out of the water'. It has an entirely different feel to it than the other tracks on the side, but its strength lies in its originality and not in the dramatics. Perhaps one of the key points to the difference in sound is the fact that it could not be created with keyboards, and she was forced to rely on Alan Murphy to create for her. She explains: ' "Waking The Witch' on side two was totally written through an electric guitarist. I knew what I wanted, but it wasn't a song that would sound right if it was based on a keyboard; it had to be written through an electric guitar. So the guitarist came in literally working to just a pattern, and I told him what I wanted. It was a very different way of writing – I'd never done it like that before – but I think it was successful. I definitely wanted to try and create a weirdness. It's all part of the second side; of the person who is in the water for the night and they have to keep going until the morning. At this point they have just woken from a dream and surfaced on the water, trying not to drown. I suppose it's the horror of being faced with something that wants to put you straight under the water again. Whether you're innocent or guilty, they're going to put you down under the water again.'

Alan Murphy remains extremely proud of the track. 'One great thing that happened in the *Hounds Of Love* for me was where I realized that Kate had learned to be completely open with something. She would now have the framework, and whereas in the past she would give me nice directives and say "Go this way" or "Go that way", she would now give me basically a framework with one or two things on it and say, "Create – do what you're going to do and I'll see if it is going to go along with what I'm going to do", and so we came up with things that were collaborations, which for me were great, especially on "Waking The Witch". That's the specific track I remember because it was such a basic track framework when we started, and yet I managed to get some things out of my playing . . . very strong sounds of my playing into the track, and yet she still managed to grab it all and put something on the top. And it's her sitting on top of the whole package that's me. That was a really nice experience – the first time that it had ever happened for us.'

No singles were released from the 'Ninth Wave'. In all likelihood this was because she had intended to make a film from the material on that side and release the singles at the same time. She did go through the motions of setting up the film, with ex-Monty Python Terry Gilliam as director. To date, this hasn't materialized. 'The Ninth Wave' opens with 'And Dream Of Sheep', a soft-sung lullaby in which the central character struggles to stay awake, realizing that to succumb to the waves would mean death, but that death is a peaceful alternative to the struggle. '*Let me be weak, let me sleep and dream of sheep*' is a simplistic but poignant appraisal of a drowning man's condition. The effort involved in his natural instinct to fight for life surmounts the pull of the waves, but he cannot imagine fighting much longer. The track leads into 'Under The Ice' where the same character imagines being on top of the water – skating on ice – only to realize that he is still in the water and trapped under the ice, a strong image of an inability to escape. Kate had written the two songs together, 'Dream Of Sheep' going straight into 'Under The Ice': they were conceived as one. 'It was very much the idea of going from very cold water, getting dark, you're alone and the only way out is to go to sleep, no responsibility, you can forget about everything. But if you go to sleep, the chances are that you could roll over in the water and drown, so you're trying to fight sleep but you can't help it and you hit the dream, and the idea of the dream being really cold and really a visual expectancy of total loneliness. For me that was a completely frozen river with no-one around, everything completely shattered with snow and icicles. It's that person all alone in that absolute cold wilderness of white and then seeing themselves under the ice drowning, when they wake up to find themselves under water.' The song is characterized by the strong cello, giving it a Jaws-like lead up which is sustained through the track, projecting a very strong sense of foreboding. 'Waking the Witch' follows, after which comes 'Watching You Without Me', a quiet but heavily synthesized production in which the drowning victim finds himself leaving his body as he returns home to his family. 'I suppose the specific message of the song,' says Kate, 'is the really horrific thought of being away from the person you love most, and there being no way you can communicate. You can't cuddle them or have the physical comfort of their physical warmth and they can't even see you or hear you. A parallel situation could exist if it was about divorce – you know, the husband coming back to see the children but he's no longer a part of the home, he's just an observer who's not seen by anyone there because his role is now different.' If the scenario is difficult to imagine, the lyrics do not clarify the situation. The general idea is supposedly conveyed by likes like, '*There's a ghost in our home . . . You didn't hear me come in/You won't hear me leaving*'. An integral part of her 'concept' is the hallucinations of a man who is on the brink of death. It is the simplest of the tracks on the 'Ninth Wave', with Paddy Bush well ensconced in the background playing balalaika, and a rich percussion backtrack.

The next and arguably the most successful track on the second side is 'Jig Of Life', another legacy of traditional Irish Music, with a very strong lyric and terrific rhythm. The Uilean pipes and fiddle of John Sheahan is not dissimilar to the instrumentation of 'Night Of The Swallow' on *The Dreaming*. John Carder Bush fills the gaps and leads into the next song with a strong narrative. Kate credits Paddy with the instrumentation and idea for the song: 'Paddy had found

125

this piece of music and said "You've just got to listen to this – its brilliant – I know you'll love it." He played it to me and instantly I wanted to use it; it was fantastic. So it was just a matter of working out a song based around the format of this piece of music he'd found. There's no doubt that Paddy was the initial inspiration, and the song is about the future person visiting the person who is in the water at that moment saying, "Look don't drown, don't die, because if you do I'm not going to be able to live my part of your life; I'm not going to have the kids that you're going to have in ten years and I'm not going to be able to move to this nice little place by the sea. So, don't die. You've got to stay alive. If not for me, then at least for yourself or your children that are to come." I suppose the suggestion of the fiddle as the devil's instrument is not unintentional. The idea of perhaps a spirit being conjured from the future – that uncanny, uncomfortable feeling of two times meeting. It's meant to be the first delivery of hope on that side of the album. There have been some very sad, disturbing experiences for the person up to this point, and although it's hardly *not* disturbing, it's meant to be a comfort – it's the future coming to rescue the present.' Eloquence in both speech and lyrics is certainly one of Kate Bush's fortés and she weaves tiny threads around the listener, drawing them into the centre of her tangled images. It is not hard to imagine a drowning, but the depths into which she winds her images indicates her very fertile imagination. She has certainly thought the whole process through and imagined what she would feel like at every toss and turn of the waves.

The next song, a strongly arranged but very traditional number, 'Hello Earth', has the protagonist stepping above the water to watch himself and the earth. He is fading from the scene, near death, *'With just one hand held up high I can blot you out/ . . . Peek-a-boo little earth.'* With a fabulous choral arrangement beneath her soft voice, the song is a rich and painful look at a man fading from his own life. The chorus swells to the sound of a megaphone calling *'All you sailors . . . Head for home'*. The choir was an ingenious addition to the song: 'It was totally inspired by a movie that I watched,' Kate recalls. 'The concept had been in my head for a couple of months and I watched this film called *Nosferatu*, directed by Friedrich Murnau and it was beautiful. There was this one piece of music that haunted me to the point where I had to use it in the song. It was exactly what I wanted to say at this point in the music, and it was building the song around that piece – it was a traditional piece that I thought was either Russian or Czechoslovakian. It is so haunting – I think a very holy piece of music in a very pure sense.'

The album culminates in the celebration of the release of the drowner from his hallucinations and his tranquil, near-death state. Morning has arrived, and with the light, new hope and safety. Through his series of experiences, he is a new man, born again in the morning fog. As with anyone who has been on the brink of death, he appreciates that much more the little things in his life which he had previously taken for granted. *'I'll kiss the ground . . . I'll tell my mother . . . my father . . . my loved one . . . my brothers/How much I love them.'* It is a fitting ending to the side and a caustic reminder to live fully. The song is a jaunty, jazzy number with several layers of her vocals swimming in and out of one another. Classic guitarist John Williams holds up the lively tempo, giving the number a credibility which offsets the slim lyrics.

As a stream-of-consciousness type lyrical ballad, the 'Ninth Wave' is effective. It is not immediately obvious that the tracks are meant to run together, and it is just as well that Kate was readily available for explanation. It is a very suitable foundation for a film track and it is obvious that she has talents in that area, something that she began to delve into in more depth later in her career. It is a soothing succession of tracks of a vastly different quality to the music of *The Dreaming*. Its simplicity and controlled vocals make it much more accessible to the listener, and by now her use of images has matured to the point where it is realistic to a degree, as in the use of hallucination as opposed to the obscure imagery that infiltrates the entirety of *The Dreaming*.

Of the five tracks on the *Hounds Of Love* side of the album, four were spawned as singles and all were successful. The album, with a distinct, and more solid percussion, had a beat that identified far more thoroughly with what was currently on the charts than anything she had produced in the past six years. When asked if she found the album more commercial than any one of her others, she noted, 'I think in some ways you're very right that it is commercial – not necessarily so intentionally as I perhaps had thought. I think the development of rhythm in my music is perhaps one of the things that makes it obviously more available to people, and there's a constancy of rhythm that perhaps wasn't there in other albums.'

Kate claims that she was not entirely responsible for the tremendous rhythms; in fact she credits her lover, Del Palmer, for his help: 'I think a very big influence there was Del. When I was initially coming up with the songs I would actually get Del to manifest in the rhythm box the pattern that I wanted. As a bass player, I think he has a very natural understanding of rhythms and working with drums, and he could also actually get the patterns that I could hear in my head and that I wanted. So it was through him that we started off with the rhythmic basis that was then built upon – it was very much what I wanted.'

She is obviously less dependent on the Fairlight in *Hounds Of Love*, appearing to be more confident of her superb vocals and the backing band's talents. The Fairlight had perhaps been overused on *The Dreaming*. Del Palmer quite obviously had more to do with the inspiration for the album than just the drum tracks. The album's theme is love, and a glowing Kate returned from her years off claiming that the powers of love had done wonderful things for her psyche. The title for the album derives from one of the tracks on the album. Kate expands: 'The Hound Of Love is an image really of someone who's afraid of being captured by love, and the imagery is of love taking the form of hounds that are hunting – so they run away because they are terrified of being caught by the hounds and ripped to shreds.' When asked if she was frightened of being caught by love, she added, 'Yes, I think so. I think everyone is. I think when you are in love with someone, you do not want to lose that and it is something that affects you in so many areas that I think it can be frightening.'

The title track uses a cello arrangement more heavily than in any of the successive tracks and disposes of the disco beat that runs through most of the A-side of the album. Her vocals are incredibly strong and deep and the lyrics contain some substantial images like, '*Take my shoes off and throw them in the lake and I'll be two steps on the water.*' The song analyses the fears that can beset anyone in love, and casts her as a fox, chased by hounds. Simon Elliot remembers Kate being most particular about her vocals on that track: 'I distinctly remember the vocal performance on it being extremely moving. She's since redone it – I'm talking about the demo. It was an

absolutely incredible vocal. I was astounded that she was considering redoing it. In fact all the vocals that she does on the demo are
always, as far as I can make out, the master vocal, but she insists on
redoing it, she's a perfectionist, but to that degree I don't see the
point.'

If 'Hounds Of Love', which was released as the third single off the
album, gave Kate a great deal of difficulty as far as vocals were
concerned, nothing matched the problems that plagued the making
of 'The Big Sky'. Kate discusses her normal process for working onto
the master tape and reflects upon how 'The Big Sky' was different: 'I
think it's finding the right avenue for the song, and in a way I think
you just have to pin down as early as you can exactly what you want
to dress the song in – you know, what colour clothes. It's very like
that, really, and you have to treat it accordingly. From the word go
the song might take on an attitude that may be completely different
from the song next to it on the album. "The Big Sky" is an example of
a real freak on the album in that it consistently changed until we got
there in the end. "The Big Sky" gave me terrible trouble really, just
as a song. You definitely do have relationships with some songs, and
we had a lot of trouble getting on together. It was just one of those
songs that kept changing, at one point every week, and it was just a
matter of trying to pin it down because it's not often I've written a
song like that where you come up with something that can literally
take you to so many different tangents, so many different forms of the
same song, that you just end up not knowing where you are with it.
That was a very strange beast.' She was, in fact, happy with the
outcome although she claims that it turned out to be very different
from the song she originally wrote. She notes philosophically:
'Maybe it's all to do with what the song is about – the fact that it was
changing all the time – the sky.'

Alan Murphy found the track quite simple. He recounts, 'I also
remember "The Big Sky". That was a nice track to do, a very open,
rocky number. The things we did went down quite nicely and easily,
but I guess Kate had to replace quite a lot of things and start from
scratch a couple of times – maybe keeping the things I had done. The
end result was a really happy kind of track.' The track is less serious
than anything else on the album, portraying a whimsical philander-
ing mood in which she simply gazes at and appreciates nature and

the grandiose spectrum of the sky. It probably isn't a bad thing to loosen up on imagery: to allow music to take precedence at times over lyric can only emphasize the rounded nature of her talents. It is a quickly-paced number, with chants, a tribal percussion and handclapping reminiscent of Gabriel, once more.

In August 1985 Kate premiered what was to be her first single from the album, 'Running Up That Hill', on BBC TV's 'Wogan', releasing the album on the same day. The single jumped immediately to number 9 in the charts and the fanfare started. The critics loved it. The fans loved it. In its first week it accumulated more hours in airplay than all the singles released from *The Dreaming* put together. More importantly, from both Kate's and EMI's points of view, she entered the US Billboard chart at number 95. She had finally found a crack in the US armour. The video for 'Running Up That Hill' was considered too risqué for the States (it featured her dancing apparently too erotically) and thus her performance on 'Wogan' was used in its place for promotional purposes.

The critics found 'Running Up That Hill' profound. Ignoring the rationale of the 'Ninth Wave', they attached themselves instead to her theory of making a deal with God, the central theme to 'Running Up That Hill'. The track is dominated by very strong percussion with no cymbals, a là Gabriel. It was an arresting theme, and one that everybody wanted to know about. Kate explains: 'It's very much about the power of love and the strength that is created between two people when they're very much in love. It's a strength that can also be threatening, violent, dangerous, as well as gentle, soothing, loving. It's saying that if these two people could swap places – if the man could become the woman and the woman the man – perhaps they would understand the feelings of that other person in a truer way, understanding it from the gender's point of view. There are very subtle differences between the sexes that can cause problems in relationships, especially when people do care about each other a lot.'

It is one of the most upbeat numbers on the album, with a rock tempo and a rich contralto. Alan Murphy felt that it was one of Kate's most successful. ' "Running Up That Hill" was the first track that I worked on when she asked me to come over and work on the album, and for me it was the biggest departure that she'd ever made. I don't think she'd ever done a track like that before and it was very interesting to play guitar because guitar fitted better into that kind of music, I felt, than anything else she'd ever done. Obviously because it fitted in better, it was easier for me to do, so we – Kate and I – started to develop something, and at that stage I just felt something happen between us and we started to work much more efficiently. So in a way I'm grateful to "Running Up That Hill" because it is what developed that feeling for us.'

The video for 'Running Up That Hill' celebrates Kate's new command of dance. She attributed much of her skill to her new dance teacher Diana Gray who whipped her back into shape after she let herself run down during the promotion of *The Dreaming*. The video features Kate and dancer Michael Hervieu, clad in grey, simple leotard, dancing to the very complex routines of director David Garfath. It is a simple video and the dance is traditional, but Kate is stunning in her mastery of movement. The filming of the video went smoothly. Unknown to Kate her co-dancer had failed to turn up for his nightly role of juggler and acrobat in *Barnum* at the Victoria Palace and was subsequently fined £400 by his union. He noted later, however, that he wouldn't have missed the chance to work with Kate Bush for anything: 'I would have asked if I could do the video,' said Hervieu, 'but I knew they would have said no.'

'Cloudbusting' was the second track to be released as a single, and was noted for its excellent, and widely acclaimed video. The song itself is based on Peter Reich's *Book Of Dreams*. She takes the point of view of the young Reich, remembering his father who was sent to prison for creating a rain machine. It is a touching tribute by a little boy to his father, with whom he shared a special relationship despite the older man's obvious eccentricity and genius. When Kate wrote the work she created the song to work both musically and visually as she had in the past, and it was consequently easily adapted to video. 'One thing that was interesting', said Kate, 'was that we had so much to say in the story visually that we extended an audio track to allow a little more room for things to be said. I think the story is very strong, and in a way it's creating images both visually and audially that say the same thing.' Kate felt very strongly about the book and asked for a plea from the public to persuade the publisher to reprint: 'It's called *A Book Of Dreams* and was written by Peter Reich.

Unfortunately the book is out of print, so I suggest that lots of people write to the publisher and demand that it's put back into print immediately. Kate portrays the young boy's voice well in the song, another sign that she anticipated the video work ahead.

The video for 'Cloudbusting' was a phenomenal success both critically and promotionally. Donald Sutherland played the part of her father in what became more of a mini-film than a vehicle for the song itself. Kate had her first real stab at acting, playing a ten-year-old Peter Reich credibly. Kate was pleased to have Donald Sutherland, 'Well, I think I'm very lucky really, he was the first choice. He was perfect. He couldn't have been better to play the part. It was a matter of finding how to contact him, but through a very nice man called Barry Richardson I managed to make contact with Donald and then asked him. And he said "Yes, I would be interested". It all went from there. It all happened very quickly. I think I must have only contacted him ten days before we started shooting and it just happened to coincide perfectly with a few days that he had off in a very busy schedule. It was brilliant. He is truly a great actor, and having watched and worked in our situation I have to reiterate that – he's just incredible, so professional and so patient. He helped me incredibly because I'd never really acted as such and I just had to react to him. He was wonderful. He puts out such an energy of sensitivity to the situation that I just had to react to him. He was, as far as I was concerned, whenever we were shooting, he was my Dad. He was wonderful.'

The story board was entirely Kate-inspired, and produced with the help of director Julian Doyle and Terry Gilliam. Because she felt so strongly about the book, she felt that the song and thus the video should have the same sort of power that the literature had for her. It took longer to make than any of her previous videos, but it was one of the first occasions on which an artist had incorporated a complete story and hired high-profile actors for a video. She goes on: 'It was fantastic to work with Julian and Terry. Everyone was so inspired by the story and everyone was moved by it, which, in a way, was one of the most important things for anyone involved in it. It was fantastic. To shoot it took about four or five days – to prepare it took about four weeks. I suppose all in all, including editing, it took about eight weeks. A long time.

Kate has since been aware of the strength of her mini-film genre of video and would like to do more work along the same lines. 'I'm starting to get a bit uncomfortable with the word video now in that I feel film is actually the media which attracts. Video was something that was great, convenient rather than ideal. I hope very much to work on film in the future.'

While the video was being filmed rumours circulated that the set was haunted by ghosts. An article in the *Daily Mirror* said: 'They had an eerie time in their four days of filming at the White Horse Hill beauty spot in Oxfordshire. A local said . . . "They found it very disturbing. They said they felt there was someone watching them all the time – but there was no-one there." . . . According to legend a ghostly blacksmith waits to shoe the horses of travellers.'

The final song on *Hounds of Love* is 'Mother Stands For Comfort', a song in which a stolid mother hides the sins of her murderous child. The track is fairly complex and Kate doesn't offer an explanation for its inspiration or, for that matter, its meaning. If one is to go by her previous autobiographical themes, then perhaps one could take this track to mean that her mother (her family) will protect her from anything, good or bad, from herself and from anyone who comes to get her. '*But she won't mind me lying*'. But it's only a theory. The song remains inaccessible despite its simple chord structure and strong percussion. It is a rather exotic fantasy, playing on perhaps a nursery rhyme or one of the traditional folk tales she draws upon so heavily. In an interview for *Melody Maker*, she noted; 'My most striking visions of reality always seem to come to me when I'm in such a strange situation that I feel "this isn't real". It's very simple really. Simplicity is a thing few people dare to go for. They think it's too easy. In fact, it's the hardest thing to do. I like the hypnotic quality of nursery rhyme repetition. A lot of traditional music has that as a basis – that something tumbling, rolling and droning throughout the piece.' Kate Bush manages to make the most simplistic images and arguments complex . . .

Hounds of Love was a startling comeback for Kate Bush, an unexpectedly colourful and marketable album from a star from whom EMI had doubted they would ever receive 'single' material again. She had fully justified the amount of time taken off to work on the album, and the construction of her own studio was obviously a clever career move. Her firm following was delighted that she was reaffirmed as Britains greatest female pop star, and picking up thousands of new fans along the way she even managed to crack the elusive USA market.

In August 1985 Kate appeared for the first time since 'Wuthering Heights' on BBC's 'Top of the Pops', singing 'Running Up That Hill'. It immediately jumped to number 3 where it remained for several weeks, going silver within a month and doubling both sales expectations for the single and sales figures for her last successful hit, 'Babooshka'. The record was launched with the traditional EMI-style extravaganza at the London Planetarium, where the whole album was played to a highly original laser show. Tony Myatt recalls: 'We went to the London Planetarium where they previewed the LP, and there the combination of lighting effects with the album – the guy who did that must have spent a lot of time putting them together, and I'm sure Kate must have been involved the whole time – but the whole thing, the sound and the lights, it was just a sensational evening, wonderful. I don't know how she does it.' Alan Murphy continues, 'She is a well of creativity, and it's only now that I think she's finding her feet. I'm not putting down anything she's done before – it's all been formulative – but now I think, especially with her studio, she's finding a system for the release of her creativity, so I think it's all going to happen from now on rather than what's gone before. Everyone has seen that she is a very creative person on all fronts, whether it's videos, dancing, stage or singing, or even playing – she has her own way of doing things from a playing point as well, but I think it's only the tip of the iceberg.'

Hounds of Love entered the official music charts on 20th September 1985. It was number 1. And that really was the tip of the iceberg. Kate Bush was back.

12
CURTAIN CALL

It wouldn't take me long
To tell you how to find it
. . . This little girl inside me
Is retreating to her favourite place.
'Under the Ivy'
Kate Bush, 1985

'Running Up That Hill' became an instant international hit, putting Kate Bush on the top of charts around the world. Critics raved that she was back, for good this time, dismissing *The Dreaming* as unrepresentative of her talents. It was as if she had never left the scene. The promotion began in earnest in September 1985 when Kate travelled again to Germany and France, choosing 'Running Up That Hill', 'Cloudbusting' and 'The Big Sky' to perform. On the other side of the ocean, the US fans were demanding her appearance, and for the first time in over six years she acquiesced. In anticipation of her visit, EMI America organized the largest ever convention of sales representatives in New Orleans in an attempt to saturate the market with her material immediately prior to her trip. They were successful. 'Hounds Of Love' entered the US Billboard Top 100 in the number 74 position. They were ready for her.

Overcoming her fear of flying, Kate agreed to fly over on Concorde despite rampant rumours in the press that she would not be promoting the album in America. One of the factors influencing her decision to fly was the fact that it was nearing the hectic Christmas season, and having a great deal more promotion to get through she couldn't afford the time it would take to sail. She set forth for the US on 17 November, an EMI executive confirming: 'she flew to New York by Concorde, and it went fine – better than we

135

thought – and she will be returning the same way.' Landing in New York City, Kate visited the Tower Records store in Greenwich Village, where she was greeted by a three block-long queue of fans. Numerous television appearances and radio interviews followed, and 'Hounds Of Love' climbed to number 30 on the Billboard charts, where it peaked.

The track from *The Ninth Wave* entitled 'Hello Earth' was featured on 'Miami Vice', the hottest cops and robbers TV programme in the US, with megastar Don Johnson in the lead. Airways were jammed in the studio after the screening of the episode. Demands to know who the artist of the song was persisted for hours, and thousands of letters were received complimenting Kate. It appeared to be the type of song that the US fans were after: a melodic, simple ballad-type number with straightforward lyrics and a strong chorus. Because in general the Americans seemed to be less patient with new attempts at Pop/Art Rock, and hadn't, in general, found the time to concentrate on the music of Kate Bush, she hadn't been able to crack the top ten, although airplay of her songs was increasing all the time. Kate remained an enigma to the American audience, despite her attempt to appear in person and force them to see that there was something to her music. The bestselling numbers in the US remain the ones with a distinct percussion running through, the livelier, more traditional rock music that can be danced to, like 'Running Up That Hill', 'Babooshka', and 'Wuthering Heights'.

In Canada, however, the album was greeted with a fabulous response. Travelling to Toronto and several other cities, Kate made several personal appearances, and was interviewed by pop king Skot Turner for CFNY FM. The Canadian all-music cable channel 'Muchmusic' played Kate's videos as part of their regular rotation, thus exposing her to a far greater section of the market. The album responded by jumping into the top 10, peaking at number 7, but remaining in the top 20 for over six weeks.

'Cloudbusting' was released in October as the second single on the album, accompanied by its smash video featuring Donald Sutherland, and rose quickly to the number 20 position on the UK charts. It peaked there, critics claim, because of Kate's refusal to perform on 'Top of the Pops'. Feeling strongly that the video was the truest representation of the song, enlivening it to its fullest potential, she asked that the BBC air it instead. EMI were furious with Kate, realizing that her performance on the show would have doubled sales almost immediately. The BBC refused to play her video, miffed that she was so stubborn, and consequently gave her position to another artist. As a result 'Cloudbusting' began its trek down the charts.

Kate returned to Germany and France in late November for a final appearance before Christmas, then came home to find that *Hounds Of Love* had turned platinum. It was her first album to record sales so quickly since *The Kick Inside*. The *Record Mirror* honoured her with two awards immediately prior to Christmas, Best Album for *Hounds Of Love* and Best Single for 'Running Up That Hill'. The exposure of Kate Bush reached peaks unknown since the first album, and the mimics were back at work.

In January 1986, Kate filled in for Sade, who was unable to appear on the British Phonographic Industry Awards, performing 'Hounds Of Love' live. She was nominated for three awards, Best Female Singer, Best Album for *Hounds Of Love* and Best Single for 'Running Up That Hill', but did not win anything much to her and her fans' disappointment. The exposure was tremendous, though, as she appeared in the star-studded gala performance which was transmitted live from London's Grosvenor House Hotel, and was simultaneously heard on London's Radio One. Annie Lennox of the Eurythmics was voted Best Female Singer, while Dire Straits, took the number one album for *Brothers In Arms*, and Tears for Fears grabbed the top single with 'Shout'. Kate won the Sounds poll for 1985, rating Best Female Vocalist of the year. Immediately afterwards 'Hounds Of Love' was released as the third single off the album. Giving in this time to a restless record company, Kate performed the single live on 'Top of the Pops' and was rewarded with its ascent to number 18 where it remained for several weeks. It was a disappointing follow up to 'Running Up That Hill', and it is generally felt that the single should have been released much earlier, before the album began to drop in the charts.

In February 1986 Kate began recording a duet with Peter Gabriel entitled 'Don't Give Up'. The song was written by Gabriel in a tumultuous period of his life, a time when he and his wife were having irreparable personal problems. It was inspired by a television programme about the effects of unemployment on relationships and home life, and by a photograph by Dorothea Lane – 'In This Proud Land' – which featured the 'dust bowl conditions in America during the Great Depression.' Although it is alleged that he had originally wanted a country star to sing with him, he turned to Kate, and they produced what was to become one of the greatest singles of 1986 and 1987. Because of the trouble with directors the video simply consists of shots of Gabriel clutching Kate to him as they revolve in front of a setting sun. Jill Gabriel, Peter's wife, later commented that it 'hurt her to watch Kate held in Peter's arms'.

There were rampant rumours at the time that Kate was having an affair with Gabriel, who had recently split with his previous lover Rosanna Arquette. At one stage it was speculated that Gabriel would finally leave his wife for Kate and that Del Palmer was in a suicidal state over the matter. The tabloids announced that Kate had moved out of her home with Del because of irreconcilable differences which were attributed to her relationship with Peter Gabriel. Kate was, however, quick to deny that they were anything more than friends, thus slashing the rumours to pieces, 'I think of him as a friend. I really admire Peter Gabriel, and I would like to work with him again in the future. We work well together and we are friends. That is all.'

The single was released in October of 1986 to an immense fanfare. The song entered the charts on 1 November, rising quickly to number 9, and it remained in the charts for 9 weeks altogether.

In March Kate appeared on the Tyne Tees TV programme, 'The Tube', in celebration of its 100th edition. She prepared a pre-recorded performance of 'Under The Ivy', otherwise known as the 'B' side to 'Running Up That Hill'. 'Under The Ivy' sounds far more like Kate's pre-*Dreaming* recordings, with simplified lyrics and the use of her favourite chord patterns. It distinctly reflects the tendency Kate has to escape the fanfare and return to her private place, which inevitably means communing with nature. '*Go into the garden/Go under the Ivy . . . To give away a secret – it's not safe.*'

Because of the demands of her time, Kate was forced to shelve plans for a movie version of 'The Ninth Wave' conceptual side of the *Hounds Of Love* album. Film work still featured in her plans, and she felt annoyed that she had had to turn down a number of very good roles because of necessary promotion for the album. The video for 'The Big Sky' was the next visual production on the cards, and in March she filmed it with the aid of over one hundred of her fans selected from fan clubs across Britain. Filming at Elstree in Hertfordshire, the video has Kate clad in a silver jumpsuit complete with parachute harness. The fans were asked to wave lights and sing along.

In April Kate took part in 'Comic Relief', a performance by comedians and singers in aid of the Ethiopian famine. Live at the Shaftesbury theatre in London, Kate participated on the first of three evenings that made up the benefit. With Del and her brother John firmly implanted in the front row of the theatre, Kate performed 'Breathing' with only her own piano as accompaniment. Her voice was clear and unhesitant, and looking fit and healthy in a fawn coloured suit she was given a seven-minute standing ovation by the crowd. There is no doubt that she was back in her position as Britain's favourite female pop star. She went on to sing a raunchy duet with Rowan Atkinson, a parody of a love song which sent the audience into gales of laughter. Other guests on the evening were Rik Mayall, Stephen Fry, Midge Ure, Bob Geldof and Paula, Pamela Stephenson and Billy Connolly. The three-night gala benefit raised hundreds of thousands of pounds for the cause and it was one of Kate's premier benefit performances. She was rather put out that she was not asked to perform in Live Aid, but rationalized that since she had not been in the charts for a number of years, and had not had a hit for at least three, it was unrealistic to expect to be included. Gabriel was not asked either. Kate remembers, 'I wasn't one of the organizers of that whole event and I think it's brilliant and made history – the amount of help they gave to people that needed it, through their music. I wasn't asked to be involved and perhaps if I had had a successful album at the time, I might have been, who knows.' When asked if she would have performed live in front of all of the people watching around the world, she was most emphatic: 'Oh most definitely. I think that anyone who didn't, who was asked, it was probably because they just couldn't, they had other commitments. I don't think anyone would say no to that.' It was odd, actually, that Bob Geldof did not include Kate in his organization, despite the fact that she had been off the scene for a while. He is a

self-proclaimed admirer. At the end of the 'Comic Relief' perform-
ance, Kate had a chance to become involved in the 'Do They Know
It's Christmas' number when the entire cast filled the stage as Bob
Geldof and Midge Ure led the vocals.

Kate was present at the Claude Gill Bookshop in Oxford Street,
London when the *Comic Relief Christmas Book* was launched, and she
signed autographs for thousands of fans along with Mel Smith, Gryf
Rhys Jones, French and Saunders and other heroes of the British
comedy club.

In October Kate released 'Experiment IV, a track she had been
working on since the beginning of *Hounds Of Love*. The song was born
during the recording of the *Hounds* album and released as a
front-runner single for her first compilation album, *The Whole Story*.
Alan Murphy recalls: 'Experiment IV was for *The Whole Story*. I'm
not sure . . . I think we were working on "Running Up That Hill"
when EMI called to say, "We've got this great idea – it's nearly
Christmas – why don't we put out a double album of all the singles.
Kate looked kind of horrified as if to say "Oh no, divine intervention
again", but it obviously was a good idea and it was quite near the
time that it should happen, and fortunately the package is so nice.
With the inclusion of the song that she developed for it, I think she
felt that it would be a worthwhile cause, so "Experiment IV" was
born. The theme was the sound experiments that went on during the
last war, you know, machines that hurt from a distance by emitting
sound waves at various frequencies, so it had a very strong theme,
and for me it was quite similar to "Running Up That Hill" in its
spirit, in that its heart was intrinsic to it – it felt very easy to play
things in the song. "Experiment Four came" together within a day, I
think.'

Four days after the release of the single, Kate appeared on BBC's
'Wogan' for the second time that year to perform live. Playing on the
comic theme which was still fresh in her mind from 'Comic Relief',
Kate asked Dawn French and Hugh Laurie of the Comic Strip
crowd to take part in her video. The result is a solid satire of
government 'top secret' experimentation. The video was shot on
location at an abandoned military hospital in South-east London.

'Comic Relief' was one of the greatest influences on Kate's life.
From this point she began to involve herself in numerous charitable

causes, becoming one of the most popular and prominent musicians in fundraising events. Having become firm friends with members of the Comic Strip, she began to incorporate a number of comic techniques in her videos. In 'Experiment IV' Kate herself appears as a vixen-like blonde ghost, floating in and around the set. It is one of Kate's most spectacular videos, a punchy satire of government secrecy. She has avoided being labelled as a 'cause' lyricist while using her extraordinary theatrics and vocal range to create a song and video that are both fundamentally socially conscious and poignant.

Always conscious of her fans, Kate interrupted the shooting of the video to attend a fan club party at London's Video Café. Members of Homeground and the Kate Bush Club were invited to meet Kate, receiving T-shirts and autographed pictures. Despite her long absences from the scene, Kate's enormous fanzines remain strong in number and continuously growing. It is interesting that Kate's fans range from the age of twelve to fifty-five! As she noted earlier in her career, her music truly has appeal for all ages. Kate Bush is one of the first females to have broken out of the strictly chart-conscious youth following to receive enormous fanfare from people of all ages. Men appear to be immensely attracted by her beauty. A male fan in a book store said 'God, I love Kate Bush,' and when asked which of her albums was his particular favourite, said, 'Oh, I hate her music, I just like her.' He claims to have every poster and piece of promotional material ever printed. Such is the diversity of her fans – she attracts both serious music lovers and appreciative males.

In November 1986 Kate released *The Whole Story*, the compilation album which featured 'Experiment IV'. EMI prepared their most expensive promotional campaign ever, flooding the media with posters, television advertisements, special radio broadcasts. The album reacted immediately. To date, it still remains on the bestselling albums and the bestselling compact discs lists. Prominently portrayed in all the record stores, Kate's album has already reached double platinum status. The success of 'Don't Give Up' with Peter Gabriel attracted more attention to Kate, making *The Whole Story* her bestselling album ever. A video was released with the album. Similar in style to 'The Single File' video, Kate has compiled the best of her single's vignettes, plus the new 'Experiment IV' video.

Kate's accomplishment is evident from the very different videos that appear on the track. Using the videos that appeared alongside each single release, Kate appears very young and quite unpolished in 'Wuthering Heights' and 'The Man With The Child In His Eyes', while the extraordinary successful 'Cloudbusting' illustrates her budding dramatic skills. Kate upgraded the vocals of 'Wuthering Heights' for the album, reducing the shrill aspects of the first recording and celebrating instead the new control over her vocal range. The resulting album is a spectacular tribute to Kate and her music, displaying the very diverse range of hits that she has had over the past ten years. Her accomplishment is undeniable. From her label as 'one-hit wonder' with 'Wuthering Heights' to the unusual and demanding *The Dreaming* and on to the mature and somehow much more commercial 'Running Up That Hill' and *Hounds of Love*, Kate has created a highly unique repertoire that has placed her in the well-deserved position of Britain's foremost female musician. And rumour has it that she has sold more posters than Samantha Fox.

'Don't Give Up' placed Kate back in the forefront of the public eye. The sensational duet with Peter Gabriel received enormous critical attention, with Kate's voice sounding extraordinarily refined and mature. Speculation about her new album immediately ensued, and fans and critics alike wondered if the new Kate Bush sound would turn out to be more melodic than it had been in the past.

The Whole Story was immensely successful in the USA, entering the Billboard 200 Album Chart at number 154. To date it remains in the charts, while Kate's video for 'The Big Sky' was nominated for the Best Video by a Female in the 1987 annual MTV video awards in the USA. Placed among Madonna and Cyndi Lauper, Kate, although she has not won an award, has established herself as one of the most accomplished video artists in the world. The video for *The Whole Story* was also immensely successful, being placed among the top three rented videos in twenty-eight states in the USA. With the hugely successful *Hounds of Love*, and more recently *The Whole Story*, Kate has finally cracked the American market.

In February 1987 'Running Up That Hill' tied with Dylan's 'Like A Rolling Stone' at the thirteenth spot in *NME*'s Top 150 singles of all time. Despite the adverse criticism, she had truly made it. The little girl with the squeaky voice has captivated the world, placing herself and her music in the higher echelons of music history. Remaining reserved and very protective of her private life, Kate has nonetheless managed to attain immense fame. She has sold her music, not herself. With only one live tour to date and not a great deal of live promotion, Kate was one of the first serious female musicians in Britain, capturing both critical acclaim and the hearts and the imagination of the world.

On 9th February 1987, Kate was awarded Best Female Singer in the sixth annual British Phonographic Industry Awards held at the Grosvenor Hotel in London. Riding high on the success of 'Don't Give Up', both Kate and Peter Gabriel captured the coveted Best Singer Awards, with Kate presenting Peter Gabriel's award herself. With only a compilation album and the duet with Gabriel released in the previous two years, Kate had still managed to hold her place as Britain's favourite female musician.

By this time Kate was hard at work on her sixth album, reputedly an up-tempo album, incorporating many of the aspects that made Hounds of Love so successful. Alan Murphy, who remains a good friend of Kate's, persuaded her to take time from her own recording to work with his own band Go West on their album track, 'The King Is Dead'. Kate also took time to record a song for the soundtrack of 'She's Having a Baby', a film directed by American John Hughes of 'Breakfast Club' fame due to be released in the UK in early 1989. Her track entitled 'This Woman's Work' is the leading song, the third track that Kate has prepared for film.

She was in demand everywhere. In early 1987 Kate was asked by Amnesty International to take part in their campaign. Alison Saunderson of Amnesty explains Kate's part in the cause: 'Every few years Amnesty puts out a campaigns poster which is basically made up of lots of photographs of celebrities. It is an attempt to show the public the strong support we have from celebrities. A few years ago, Kate Bush agreed to let us use her photo in that literature and we have used it over and over again. More recently than that she was approached by Paul Gambaccini, who is a strong supporter of Amnesty, to take part in "The Secret Policeman's Third Ball" which was the third in a series of rock and comedy reviews that we do in a West End theatre in London, and we very gratefully accepted what she did for us. She agreed to perform with members of Pink Floyd,

143

and she did two tracks, "Running Up That Hill" and "Let It Be" and she did them excellently. Then she agreed to let us use them on film, record, books – any product. She contributed a great deal. Paul put all the music together. I know Dave Gilmour discovered Kate when she was only sixteen and they have had a special musical regard for one another since that time. It really was quite a coup for us to have them appearing together on stage – and with Nick Mason, also of Pink Floyd. We have something coming up in June 1988 in Milton Keynes. I know Kate is working on her current album and is very very busy, but we are hoping she will take part as she did in the past.' Kate did not take part, however, due to the demands her new album was making on her time.

'The Secret Policeman's Third Ball' was an enormous success. Beginning on 27th March 1987, it ran for four nights at the London Palladium, where Kate had appeared numerous times before, both in her own concerts and for Comic Relief and the Prince's Trust. Tickets were £25 each, and were sold out well in advance. Two of the four evenings were devoted to comedy and the other two to music. Kate agreed to play on both evenings, capturing a great deal of media attention. Gabriel, Lou Reed, Bob Geldof, Ben Elton and Joan Armatrading were only part of the star-studded line-up, while comic regulars Hale and Pace, Stephen Fry, Hugh Laurie, Spitting Image, Mel Smith and Griff Rhys Jones took part in the comedy evenings. The performances were an outstanding success raising hundreds of thousands of pounds for Amnesty. With a cunningly organized TV showing, record, film, video and the book, published by Sidgwick and Jackson in London, Amnesty is expected to make over one million pounds from the four evenings.

Then it was back to her studio. With the date for the release of her sixth album changing monthly and no title finalized, Kate's fans wait in anticipation for what is purported to be the best album yet. Working from her own studio as she had on *Hounds Of Love*, Kate has been involved in the final mixing for over six months. Kate has produced the album herself and, as has always been the case in the past, she has refused to comment on the content or the style of the album. Kate's albums have always all been unique, and expectations for the sixth album have been mounting since she finished the promotion for *The Whole Story*.

In an interview with her fan club – The Kate Bush Club – Kate notes her feelings about the recording of the new album, 'Again I am working straight onto master tape in our home studio . . . I try and keep the performances quick and spontaneous . . . I'm using the Fairlight again and a DX7 but a lot of the songs have been written on piano initially and it does definitely give the songs a different flavour from those written on Fairlight. A lot of the rhythms are arranged by Del . . . I am using a lot of real instruments on this album.' She refused to comment on the date for the release of the album but EMI are hoping for an early 1989 date.

After her work with Amnesty International and her appearances for 'Don't Give Up', Kate disappeared from the scene. Again rumours began to infiltrate the tabloids. On 28th June 1987, Kate appeared as a surprise guest at Peter Gabriel's live performance at Earl's Court in London to accompany him with 'Don't Give Up'. The applause was astounding. Kate appeared in ill-fitted clothing which again provoked speculation that she was pregnant, thus explaining her disappearance from the scene. No baby has yet appeared, but the rumours have not abated.

Since Earls Court little has been heard from Kate Bush. It is something that the fans have come to expect, however, and the resulting album has usually proved worth the wait. Kate is one of the only artists who has been able to disappear so entirely from the public eye and then manage to enter the charts at number one. Her high-profile albums have always been able to counter her low-profile persona.

Kate Bush has remained an enigma. Stunning critics and fans alike, with her quaint, unobtrusive manner she has accomplished more than any other British female musician in the short time she has been on the scene. Protected by her family, her friends, her enormously loyal fans and record company, Kate has been given the freedom to create in her own time and under her own highly structured ambitions. She entered the pop scene at sixteen, taking her first single to number one, and she hasn't looked back since. Her success is phenomenal. From an ordinary, middle-class background, the daughter of a family doctor has managed to head charts around the world, lead by her intuitive imagination and innumerable talents.

She is still the good girl of pop. Despite the rumours about her

145

sexuality, her affairs, her drug habits, she has managed to keep her life and reputation clean and clear of any scandal. She's something of a mystery, a woman with the obvious faculties of a genius, and the demeanour of a naïve child. Her life has been sheltered, but in no way is she still a child. Her infrequent interviews have shown her to be both honest and mature about her womanhood. And she has more than capably directed her own career, taking control from EMI to set up her own companies, led by the people she trusts and has chosen herself.

She has been extraordinarily successful and yet the critics remained baffled. No one can quite grasp what her attraction is. None of her songs are remotely similar to what surrounds her in the charts. Her personal promotion is very obviously unspectacular. Her lyrics are obscure and often play on stereotypical themes. She refuses to allow sexual exploitation of either herself or her image. She retains an aura of sexuality, which only feeds the enigma that surrounds her. And yet she doesn't take drugs, drink, lead the traditional 'wild life' of the enormously popular star. How the hell does she do it? With an ordinary education, an intelligent, but in every way average, family and family life, she has literally pulled herself from virtual obscurity to become one of the greatest success stories the music world has yet to see.

What is her charm? Is it the seclusion – the mystery that surrounds her – that attracts so much attention? How can such unusual, phenomenally complex music find its way into the charts with the likes of Madonna and Bananarama stealing the scene? She is vastly different in every way from any of the other female musicians that line the charts, but every time she returns to the scene, she races right back to the top, and she steals the limelight from them all. It's incredibly difficult to pinpoint what makes Kate Bush so successful.

A study of her life offers no clues as to how she has really captured the hearts of a nation and then the world. It just seems too straightforward, too simple to be true. There are no hidden sides to Kate Bush. She is a normal, healthy woman, with what appears to be absolutely natural aspirations and ambitions. She cooks her own meals, lives simply, and allows her life to revolve around her music. She has never been called anything but cordial, and in the opinion of

146

her friends and colleagues, she is an incredibly likeable young lady. She's lovely to look at, there are no lines of hardship on her elfin face and she smiles prettily in the face of even the rudest questions.

Kate Bush celebrated her thirtieth birthday this year. She looks twenty-one. The energy and the emotion that she incorporates into her music have not ravaged her in any way. Her involvement in her work is total – her phenomenal lyrics, original instrumentation, obscure production and fascinating stage presence have labelled her as a force in the music world. Like her or hate her, you just cannot ignore her. Kate Bush has single-handedly changed what is expected of female musicians. Gone are the preconceptions that a woman in the music industry must be lewd, sexy and mindless. Kate Bush is a serious musican. An albums artist with little or no regard for the contemporary charts. Perhaps it is the feeling, the intensity with which she infuses her music that is so compelling.

Her aspirations include film work and there is no denying that she will be a success. She has been a success at every single thing she has attempted, from her videos to her live performances. Kate Bush thrives on perfection, the perfection of her music and of herself and her image as a whole. She has accomplished numerous forms of dance, mime and the more complete maturity of her vocals and her lyrics.

Her life has been a success story and yet she has remained untouched. With the records she now holds she could go on forever. Maybe she will. Whatever Kate Bush does next, you can guarantee it will be worth waiting for. She's the master of her art and one of the most influential women in the last two decades of music history. She's certainly doing something right.

DISCOGRAPHY

THE BRITISH SINGLES

Wuthering Heights c/w **Kite**
EMI 2719
No. 1 Gold
Released 11th January 1978
Produced by Andrew Powell

The Man With The Child In His Eyes (single version)
c/w **Moving**
EMI 2806
No. 6
Released 28th May 1978
A-side Produced by Andrew Powell
Executive Producer Dave Gilmour
B-side Produced by Andrew Powell

Hammer Horror c/w **Coffee Homeground**
EMI 2887
No. 44
Released 27th October 1978
Produced by Andrew Powell
Assisted by Kate

Wow c/w **Fullhouse**
EMI 2911
No. 14
Released 9th March 1979
Produced by Andrew Powell
Assisted by Kate

Breathing c/w **The Empty Bullring**
EMI 5058
No. 16
Released 14th April 1980
Produced by Kate and Jon Kelly

Babooshka c/w **Ran-Tan Waltz**
EMI 5085
No. 5 Silver
Released 23rd June 1980
Produced by Kate and Jon Kelly

Army Dreamers (single remix)
c/w **Delius** and **Passing Through Air**
EMI 5106
No. 16
Released 22nd September 1980
A-side Produced by Kate and Jon Kelly
B-side (1) Produced by Kate and Jon Kelly
B-side (2) Produced by Dave Gilmour

December Will Be Magic Again c/w **Warm And Soothing**
EMI 5121
No. 29
Released 17th November 1980
A-side Produced by Kate and Jon Kelly
B-side Produced by Kate

Sat In Your Lap c/w **Lord Of The Reedy River**
EMI 5201
No. 11
Released 29th June 1981
Produced by Kate
B-side written by Donovan

The Dreaming c/w **Dreamtime** (instrumental version)
EMI 5296
No. 48
Released 26th July 1982
Produced by Kate

There Goes A Tenner c/w **Ne T'en Fui Pas**
EMI 5350
Did not chart
Released 2nd November 1982
Produced by Kate

Running Up That Hill c/w **Under The Ivy**
KB1
No. 3 Silver
Released 5th August 1985
Produced by Kate

Cloudbusting c/w **Burning Bridge**
KB2
No. 20
Released 14th October 1985
Produced by Kate

Hounds Of Love c/w **The Handsome Cabin Boy**
KB3
No. 18
Released 17th February 1986
Produced by Kate
B-side Traditional

The Big Sky (special single mix) c/w **Not This Time**
KB4
KB4P (Limited Edition Picture Disc)
No. 37
Released 28th April 1986
Produced by Kate

Experiment IV c/w **Wuthering Heights** (new vocal)
KB5
No. 23
Released 27th October 1986
A-side Produced by Kate
B-side Produced by Andrew Powell
Remix by Jim Parton

THE BRITISH EP

Kate Bush Live On Stage
MIEP 2991
No. 10
Released 3rd September 1979
Produced by Kate and Jon Kelly
Promotional Double Single
PSR 442 and PSR 443
Tracks:
Them Heavy People
Don't Push Your Foot On The Heartbrake
James And The Cold Gun
L'Amour Looks Something Like You

THE BRITISH 12-INCH SINGLES

Running Up That Hill (12-inch remix)
c/w **Running Up That Hill** (Instrumental Version)
and **Under The Ivy**
12KB1
Released 5th August 1985
Produced by Kate

Cloudbusting (The Orgonon Mix)
c/w **Burning Bridge** and **My Lagan Love**
12KB2
Released 14th October 1985
Produced by Kate

Alternative Hounds Of Love
c/w **The Handsome Cabin Boy** and **Jig Of Life**
12KB3
Released 17th February 1986
Produced by Kate

The Big Sky (The Meteorological Mix)
c/w **Not This Time** and **The Morning Fog**
12KB4
Released 28th April 1986
Produced by Kate

Experiment IV (12-inch Remix)
c/w **Wuthering Heights** (New Vocal) and
December Will Be Magic Again
12KB5
Released 3rd November 1986
Produced by Kate

THE ALBUMS

The Kick Inside
EMC 3223
No. 3 Triple Platinum
Limited Edition Picture Disc
EMCP 3223
Released 17th February 1978

MOVING
SAXOPHONE SONG*
STRANGE PHENOMENA
KITE
THE MAN WITH THE CHILD IN HIS EYES*
WUTHERING HEIGHTS
JAMES AND THE COLD GUN
FEEL IT
OH TO BE IN LOVE
L'AMOUR LOOKS SOMETHING LIKE YOU
THEM HEAVY PEOPLE
ROOM FOR THE LIFE
THE KICK INSIDE

*Recorded June 1975 AIR Studios, London.
Executive Producer Dave Gilmour, Arranger Andrew Powell,
Engineer Geoff Emerick.

Musicians: Andrew Powell piano, Barry De Souza drums, Paul Keogh acoustic and electric guitar, Bruce Lynch bass, Alan Parker guitar, Alan Skidmore saxophone.

Remainder recorded August to October 1977 AIR Studios, London. Producer Andrew Powell, Engineer Jon Kelly.

Musicians: Ian Bairnson guitar, backing vocals, beer bottles, Paddy Bush mandolin, backing vocals, Stuart Elliot drums, percussion, Duncan Mackay electric piano, synthesizer, organ, clarinet, David Paton bass, backing vocals, Morris Pert percussion, boobams, Andrew Powell celeste bass, electric piano, beer bottles.

Lionheart
EMA 787
No. 6 Gold
Released 10th November 1978

SYMPHONY IN BLUE
IN SEARCH OF PETER PAN
WOW
DON'T PUSH YOUR FOOT ON THE HEARTBRAKE
OH ENGLAND MY LIONHEART
FULLHOUSE
IN THE WARM ROOM
KASHKA FROM BAGHDAD
COFFEE HOMEGROUND
HAMMER HORROR

Recorded July to August 1978 at Superbear Studios, Nice, France. Produced by Andrew Powell, assisted by Kate, Engineer Jon Kelly.

Musicians: Ian Bairnson electric guitar, rhythm guitar, Fender Rhodes, Brian Bath guitar, Paddy Bush mandolin, mandocello, pan pipes, slide guitar, strumento de porco, Stuart Elliot drums, percussion, Richard Harvey recorders, Duncan Mackay acoustic and electric guitar, synthesizer, Fender Rhodes, Francis Monkman Hammond harpsichord, Charlie Morgan drums, Del Palmer bass, David Paton bass, Andrew Powell joanna strumentum harmonium.

Never For Ever
EMA 794
No. 1 Platinum
Released 8th September 1980

BABOOSHKA
DELIUS
BLOW AWAY*
ALL WE EVER LOOK FOR
EGYPT*
THE WEDDING LIST*
VIOLIN*
THE INFANT KISS
NIGHT SCENTED STOCK
ARMY DREAMERS
BREATHING (Album Re-mix)

*Recorded Autumn-Winter 1979 at AIR studios, London.
Produced by Kate and Jon Kelly, Engineer Jon Kelly.

Musicians: Brian Bath acoustic and electric guitar, backing vocals, Kevin Burke violin, Paddy Bush banshee, strumento de porco, musical saw, harmonica, backing vocals, Preston Heyman drums, percussion, backing vocals, Martin Ford, orchestra strings, Max Middleton Fender Rhodes, Minimoog, Mike Moran Prophet 5, Alan Murphy electric guitar, Del Palmer fretless bass, electric bass.

Remainder recorded January to June 1980 at Abbey Road Studios, London.
Produced by Kate and Jon Kelly, Engineer Jon Kelly.

Musicians: Ian Bairnson backing vocals, Brian Bath electric and acoustic guitar, Andrew Bryant backing vocals, Paddy Bush balalaika, sitar, koto, mandolin, backing vocals, Stuart Elliot drums, bodhran, Larry Fast Prophet 5, John Giblin bass, fretless bass, Roy Harper backing vocals, Preston Heyman percussion, backing vocals, Gary Hurst backing vocals, Duncan Mackay Fairlight CMI, Max Middleton Fender Rhodes, Alan Murphy electric and acoustic guitar, bass acoustic guitar, Jo and Adam Sceaping livoni, viol and string arrangements.

Fairlight CMI programming by Richard Burgess and John Walters.

The Dreaming
EMC 3419
No. 3 Gold
Released 13th September 1982

SAT IN YOUR LAP (Album Re-mix)
THERE GOES A TENNER
PULL OUT THE PIN
SUSPENDED IN GAFFA
LEAVE IT OPEN
THE DREAMING
NIGHT OF THE SWALLOW
ALL THE LOVE
HOUDINI
GET OUT OF MY HOUSE

Recorded as follows: May 1981 at Townhouse Studios, Produced by Kate, Engineer Hugh Padgham. May to June 1981 at Townhouse Studios, Produced by Kate, Engineer Nick Launay. June 1981 at Abbey Road Studios, Produced by Kate, Engineer Haydn Bendall. August to December 1981 at Oddesey Studios, Produced by Kate, Engineer Paul Hardiman. January to May 1982 at Advision Studios, Produced by Kate, Engineer Paul Hardiman.

Backing tracks and overdubs for NIGHT OF THE SWALLOW recorded at Windmill Lane Studios, Dublin, July 1981.

Final mix at Advision Studios, Produced by Kate, Engineer Paul Hardiman, Assistant Engineer David Taylor, Digital Editor Peter Woolliscroft.

Musicians: Stewart Arnold backing vocals, Jimmy Bain bass, Ian Bairnson acoustic guitar, backing vocals, Brian Bath electric guitar, Paddy Bush sticks, strings, mandolins, bullroarer, backing vocals, Geoff Downes Fairlight CMI, brass, Percy Edwards animal noises, Stuart Elliot drums, percussion, sticks, Dave Gilmour backing vocals, Gosfield Goers crowd noises, Paul Hardiman backing vocals, Rolf Harris didgeridoo, Gary Hurst backing vocals, Sean Keane fiddle, David Lawson synclavier, string arrangement on Houdini, Donnal Lunny bouzouki, Alan Murphy electric guitar, Liam O'Flynn uillean pipes, penny whistle, Del Palmer fretless bass, 8-string bass, bass, backing vocals, Esmail Sheikh drum talk, Danny Thompson string bass, Richard Thornton boy soprano, Eberhard Weber bass, Bill Whelan pipe and string arrangement on 'Night of the Swallow'.

Hounds Of Love
KAB 1
No. 1 Double Platinum
Released 16th September 1985

RUNNING UP THAT HILL
HOUNDS OF LOVE
THE BIG SKY
MOTHER STANDS FOR COMFORT
CLOUDBUSTING
THE NINTH WAVE
AND DREAM OF SHEEP
UNDER ICE
WAKING THE WITCH
WATCHING YOU WITHOUT ME
JIG OF LIFE
HELLO EARTH
THE MORNING FOG

(Tape cassette version contains additionally 'Running Up That Hill' 12-inch Re-mix).

Recorded January 1984 to June 1985 at Kate's own studio in Kent. Produced by Kate, Engineered by Del Palmer, Haydn Bendall, Brian Tench, Paul Hardiman, Nigel Walker, and James Guthrie.

Backing tracks and overdubs for JIG OF LIFE recorded at Windmill Lane Studios, Dublin, Produced by Kate, Engineer Bill Somerville-Large.

Final mix by Brian Tench and Julian Mendelsohn.

Musicians: Brian Bath guitar, backing vocals, Michael Berkeley arranged choir on HELLO EARTH, John Carder Bush narration, backing vocals, Paddy Bush balalaika, didgeridoo, violin, fugare, backing vocals, Stuart Elliot drums, Richard Hickox direction of choir on HELLO EARTH, Michael Kaman orchestral arrangements, Dave Lawson string arrangement on CLOUDBUSTING, Donnal Lunny bouzouki bodhran, Kevin McAlea Fairlight CMI sequences, synthesizer, Charlie Morgan drums, handclaps, Alan Murphy guitar, Liam O'Flynn uilean pipes, Del Palmer bass, Fairlight CMI bass, handclaps, Morris Pert percussion, Richard Hickox Singers choir, John Sheahan fiddles, whistles, Danny Thompson double bass, Eberhard Weber bass, John Williams guitar, Jonathan Williams cello, Bill Whelan Irish arrangements, Youth bass.

The Whole Story (Compilation)
KBTV1
Released 10th November 1986

WUTHERING HEIGHTS (New Vocal)
CLOUDBUSTING
THE MAN WITH THE CHILD IN HIS EYES
BREATHING
WOW
HOUNDS OF LOVE
RUNNING UP THAT HILL
ARMY DREAMERS
SAT IN YOUR LAP
EXPERIMENT IV
THE DREAMING
BABOOSHKA

EXPERIMENT IV recorded at Kate's own Studio in Kent, Summer 1986. Produced by Kate.

Musicians on 'Experiment IV': Stuart Elliot drums, Nigel Kennedy violin, Alan Murphy guitar.

Note: The only tracks not available on official British release are the French language version of THE INFANT KISS entitled UN BAISER D'ENFANT and the remixed version of NE T'EN FUI PAS. These are available on overseas releases as follows:

Ne T'en Fui Pas c/w **Un Baiser D'Enfant**
Pathe Marconi EMI (France)
EMI 5444

Ne T'en Fui Pas c/w **Dreamtime**
EMI America (Canada)
72917

Un Baiser D'Enfant c/w **Suspended in Gaffa**
EMI America (Canada)
72931

Kate Bush (Mini-LP)
SAT IN YOUR LAP
JAMES AND THE COLD GUN
BABOOSHKA
SUSPENDED IN GAFFA
UN BAISER D'ENFANT
EMI America (USA)
MLP 19004

Kate Bush (Mini-LP)
SAT IN YOUR LAP
JAMES AND THE COLD GUN
NE T'EN FUI PAS
BABOOSHKA
SUSPENDED IN GAFFA
UN BAISER D'ENFANT
EMI America (Canada)
MLP 19004

Kate's Session Work With Other Artists

Leslie Duncan
Sing Children Sing
CBS CBS 8061

Peter Gabriel
Peter Gabriel (Third solo album)
Charisma CDS 4019
Tracks: **Games Without Frontiers**
Charisma CB 354
   No Self Control
Charisma CB 360

Roy Harper
The Unknown Soldier
Harvest SHVL 820
Tracks: **You (The Game Part III)**

Ray Shell
Them Heavy People
EMI EMI 5142

Zaine Griff
Figures
Polydor POLO 5061
Tracks: **Flowers**
Polydor POSP 506

Peter Gabriel
So
Charisma/Virgin PG5
Tracks: **Don't Give Up**
Charisma/Virgin PGS 2

Big Country
The Seer
Phonogram
Tracks: **The Seer**

Go West
Dancing On The Couch
Chrysalis GOW6
Tracks: **The King Is Dead**
Chrysalis CDL 1550

Various Artists
Greenpeace: The Album
Tower Bell Records FUND 1
Tracks: **Breathing**

Various Artists
The Secret Policeman's Third Ball
Virgin V2458
Tracks: **Running Up That Hill**